NOV 2 1 2018

Reading to Write: A Textbook of Advanced Chinese

D0025935

Traditionally, reading and writing are believed to be separate but related language processes and teachers follow the conventional wisdom of teaching in-depth reading, with writing as a tag-on issue.

Therefore, there exists an increasingly urgent call for a well-rounded reading-writing curriculum and a theoretically-informed, empirically-based, student-centered advanced textbook that aims to develop the synergy between reading and writing. *Reading to Write: A Textbook of Advanced Chinese* is intended to fill this significant gap. It treats reading and writing as integrative parts and interactive skills in Chinese language teaching, putting them hand-in-hand, supplementing each other.

Zu-yan Chen is a Professor of Chinese Language and Literature at Binghamton University, State University of New York. He holds the rank of SUNY Distinguished Teaching Professor. His publications include seven books and many articles spanning the fields of literature, history, philosophy, and language pedagogy.

Reading to Write: A Textbook of Advanced Chinese

高级中文读写教程

Zu-yan Chen

Routledge
Taylor & Francis Group

LONDON AND NEW YORK

First published 2019
by Routledge
2 Park Square, Milton Park, Abingdon, Oxon OX14 4RN

and by Routledge
711 Third Avenue, New York, NY 10017

Routledge is an imprint of the Taylor & Francis Group, an informa business

© 2019 Zu-yan Chen

The right of Zu-yan Chen to be identified as author of this work has been asserted by him in accordance with sections 77 and 78 of the Copyright, Designs and Patents Act 1988.

All rights reserved. No part of this book may be reprinted or reproduced or utilised in any form or by any electronic, mechanical, or other means, now known or hereafter invented, including photocopying and recording, or in any information storage or retrieval system, without permission in writing from the publishers.

Trademark notice: Product or corporate names may be trademarks or registered trademarks, and are used only for identification and explanation without intent to infringe.

British Library Cataloguing-in-Publication Data
A catalogue record for this book is available from the British Library

Library of Congress Cataloging-in-Publication Data
A catalog record has been requested for this book

ISBN: 978-1-138-54380-5 (hbk)
ISBN: 978-1-138-54381-2 (pbk)
ISBN: 978-1-351-00590-6 (ebk)

Typeset in Times New Roman
by Apex CoVantage, LLC

Printed and bound by CPI Group (UK) Ltd, Croydon, CR0 4YY

Contents 目录

Acknowledgements 鸣谢

Looking back at the long and richly rewarding process of writing this book, I would like to thank Stephanie Hosier for her excellent assistance in editing the English translation of the texts. Working with Stephanie has resulted in a translation in which both literal and literary renderings – two arguably conflicting styles of interpretation – were carefully attended to and skillfully balanced throughout this textbook.

I am also profoundly indebted to my wife and colleague Hong Zhang, who has used this manuscript for her Advanced Chinese class in a field test at Binghamton University. The feedback from her students and herself contributed significantly to the revision process. I am grateful to Hong for her patience, enthusiasm, and love; for these I would like to dedicate this book to her.

Preface 前言

> Read ten thousand volumes, 读书破万卷
> Write as if divine. 下笔如有神
>
> ——Du Fu

These two famous lines by Du Fu (712–770), one of the greatest poets in Chinese history, address the connection between reading and writing. Although Du Fu mainly focused on poetry writing, this connection nevertheless plays a similar role in literacy and foreign language education, even after 12 centuries. Reading and writing are processes that are interdependent, yet mutually beneficial. However, in practice, many instructors of Chinese as a foreign language follow the conventional wisdom of teaching in-depth reading, while treating writing as an afterthought. Some instructors, even at the advanced levels, only ask students to write sentences or short paragraphs. As a result, students often perceive reading as a decoding process and writing as only a task of constructing grammatically correct sentences. Therefore, there exists an increasingly urgent call for a well-rounded reading-writing curriculum and a theoretically informed, empirically based and student-centered advanced textbook that aims to develop the synergy of reading and writing.

Reading to Write: A Textbook for Advanced Chinese is thus intended to fill this significant gap. It treats reading and writing as integrative parts and interactive skills as a whole in Chinese language teaching, making them go hand-in-hand and supplement each other. Each lesson of this book is a natural marriage of reading and writing. Through reading, students are given opportunities to acquire knowledge of vocabulary, grammatical structures and rhetorical features of texts. Furthermore, reading reveals mastery of written structures, provides access to ideas, and makes students aware of how genres and patterns shape ideas. The intensive writing assignments, in turn, help students use appropriate vocabulary, apply fitting structures to paragraphs, and effectively communicate through writing. At the same time, the skills of organizing thoughts and developing the subject boost reading comprehension. This synergistic relationship of reading and writing enhances students' facility in both disciplines.

This book takes a unique approach that is genre-based and process-focused. Reading and writing are essentially social acts: one usually writes to communicate with an audience, who has expectations for the type of text, or genre, to be produced. Reading a variety of genres helps students learn text structures and language that they can then transfer to their own writing. The seven lessons in this book deal with the five most practical genres: writing about events, writing about characters, writing about scenery, writing about feelings, and finally, persuasive writing. Each of these genres serves its own purposes, follows its own rules, and has its own unique characteristics. By proceeding through these lessons, students are expected to raise their awareness of both the rhetorical organization and linguistic features associated with these genres, and to improve their ability to produce effective pieces in each category.

Coherent, engaging, and purposeful reading and writing pertaining to these genres can only be achieved through a carefully designed learning process. However, in many classes, the teaching of reading and writing, especially the latter, is not process-focused but product-oriented. A common sequence proceeds as such: the instructor gives a composition topic to students; students simply write everything they know about the topic in a disorganized and haphazard manner; the instructor then spends long hours providing feedback on the students' writing. In this trilogy, teachers and students alike both suffer death by the red pen, and writing is invariably seen as a tedious chore for all involved. It is also well-known in the folk wisdom of classrooms that students often scan through the teacher's corrections to find the final grade. Counteracting that convention, this textbook considers both reading and writing as processes in which students interact with texts meaningfully and focus on both process and product: not only on what the student produces, but more importantly, also on how to produce it.

With a process-focused approach, this book emphasizes the improvement of students' ability in constructing meaning and organizing structure in reading and writing. Foreign language students tend to tackle reading as if decoding a script and focus their attention on correcting language errors in their own writing while ignoring problems with the actual content of the texts. It is particularly important to make students aware of the significance of attending simultaneously to process and product as well as revising their own writing for a global meaning, not just for the local language problems. Hence, each lesson in this book includes one "intensive reading" 精读 text and four "extensive reading" 泛读 texts.

The **Model Text**, which is the only "intensive reading" text of a chapter, exhibits the structural, rhetorical, and linguistic features of the particular genre examined in the respective chapter. These texts are original, engaging, and relevant to students' interests and life experiences. The model text features analytical comments in the right column which help students understand how the text is organized, how the ideas are connected, and how sentences and paragraphs stay focused on the topic. With these comments, the reading process becomes much more active.

Revolving around the Model Text are three interrelated phases of instruction: Writing Guide, Rhetoric, and Commentary. These "extensive reading" texts provide a series of instructions for the reading and writing of a certain genre.

- **Writing Guide** frames the task, discussing a particular genre, its organization, suitable conventions, and stylistic features. It offers higher order questioning strategies, such as analysis, synthesis, and evaluation which help the reader and writer see beyond the obvious and explore issues in depth. It also teaches, wherever necessary, the knowledge of organizing through chronology, cause-effect, problem-solution, or reason-evidence rhetorical patterns which assist both reader and writer to recognize and apply reasoning strategies.
- **Commentary** analyzes the model text, evaluating its effectiveness, coherence, and language accuracy and articulacy. It illustrates how the model text maintains the reader's attention through interesting content, inviting writing style, effective word choice, and sentence variety.
- **Rhetoric** highlights specific literary devices from the model texts for potential incorporation into the students' writing. The seven lessons include the following topics:

Personification, Metaphor and Simile; Parallelism, Exaggeration, Association, Imagination, and Rhetorical Question.

In addition, each lesson also contains a section of **Practical Writing**. This supplementary "extensive reading" text engages students in writing for a practical purpose. The seven lessons offer instructions on the following topics: Email, Congratulatory Words, Thank-you Note, Poster, Cover Letter for Job Application, Résumé, and Reader Response.

Accordingly, the exercises of this book are designed with the approach of procedural facilitation, guiding students through a step-by-step process of writing training. The exercises are composed of three parts: Vocabulary Training, Phrase Training, and Composition Training. Not only do these exercises provide students with bits of language that they can use to fill in the linguistic holes in their texts, but they also help students pick up tricks of the literary trade. In the third part, Composition Training, writing assignments are creative and progressive in nature, and include Imitative Composition, Situational Composition, Chain Story Composition, Sequential Composition, and Practical Writing.

- **Imitative Composition** allows students to write in an efficient way based on the writing strategies illustrated in the Model Texts. Students can either write new pieces or revise previous pieces of writing, emulating the authors' techniques. Recognizing the author's rhetorical organization, grammatical patterns, transitional words and use of writing techniques such as repetition, parallelism, and summary will facilitate comprehension and communication.
- **Situational Composition** teaches students to conceptualize and formulate texts effectively from a clearly presented situation. This calls for a good understanding of the purpose of the task as well as a clear awareness of the situation and audience. All the required points should be addressed in detail, fully amplified and well-organized.
- **Chain Story Composition** is a game utilizing an electronic medium in which students take turns writing a sentence, therefore together developing a logical and interesting story. Students practice how ideas are generated, expanded, and refined through collective work. Students also establish voice and audience as well as a sense of community. This is a fantastic expectation to promote in classrooms: what I write is not only to satisfy my teacher's assignments but is also to be read by my peers.
- **Sequential Composition** is an inventive and coherent sequence of logically arranged and related writing tasks that facilitate the students' development of writing skills in both length and depth. Many students have no idea how to "fill" one to two pages. This practice will guide students through a step by step process, from writing paragraphs as organic segments to connecting them into a unified composition.

This genre-based and process-focused approach to teaching advanced Chinese reading and writing is inspired by real-life classroom experiences and is proven to be fun and easy to implement. This book demonstrates that reading and writing assignments do not have to be intimidating—for either the instructors or the students. Activities that generate and organize ideas, as well as draft and revise texts, reward students with new insights into how texts function with regard to content, organization, coherence, and style. As a result, their reading will shift from a decoding state of mind to active interpretation, and their writing will gradually shed its speech-like qualities, increasing in syntactic complexity and lexical density. In short, this textbook teaches integrated reading and writing strategies which allow teachers and students to "kill two birds with one stone."

前言

> 读书破万卷,
> 下笔如有神。
> ——杜甫

中国历史上最伟大的诗人之一杜甫的这一联名句点明了阅读与写作的关系。虽然杜甫主要着眼于诗歌创作,但此种关系甚至在历经十二个世纪后的语文和外语教学中仍至关重要。阅读与写作是互相依赖并互助互补的过程。但在实践中,很多教外国学生的中文老师习惯成自然地教深度的阅读,而仅把写作作为一种反馈。甚至有些高年级的中文老师也只让学生写短句和段落。由此而产生的结果是,学生经常把阅读作为一种"解码"过程,而写作只是建构语法正确的句子的尝试。因此,全面的阅读写作课程以及以理论为指导、以经验为基础和以学生为中心的,充分发挥阅读和写作的协力优势的高级中文教科书,已成为一种日益紧迫的需要。

《高级中文读写教程》意在填补这个重大的空白。它把阅读和写作视为中文教学中的有机组成部分和互动技能,使他们同步发展并互相补充。本书的每一课都是阅读和写作的自然结合。通过阅读,学生能获得课文中有关词汇、语法结构和修辞特色的知识。更进一步,阅读揭示写作结构、活跃思路,并使学生认识到写作体裁和模式乃塑造思想之利器。另一方面,强化的写作作业有助于学生得心应手地遣词造句,并有效地用写作来交际。同时,整理思路和发展主题的技巧也有助于提高阅读理解力。这种阅读和写作的协力优势加强学生在两个领域的能力。

本书的与众不同之处是着眼于体裁,注重于过程。阅读与写作本质上是社会行为:写作是为了跟读者交流,而读者对文章的体裁有所期待。不同体裁的阅读有助于学生学到能为己所用的文章结构和语言。本书的七课包括了五个最实用的体裁:记事、写人、绘景、抒情和议论。每一种体裁自成规矩并各具特色。逐课读来,学生自会了解到跟这些体裁相关的修辞结构和语言特色,并提高写作不同体裁作品的能力。

环环相扣、引人入胜和目的明确的阅读与写作这些体裁的文章唯有通过规划周详的学习过程才能获得。然而,在很多教室里,在阅读与写作的教学中,特别是后者,过程常被忽略,重视的只是结果。这样的情况屡见不鲜:教师出作文题目,学生随意写出对这个题目所知的一切,老师随后煞费苦心地给学生的作文写评语。在这个三部曲中,教师和学生都饱受红笔的折磨,写作不可避免的被所有相关的人觉得是令人生厌的繁琐之事。何况心照不宣却尽人皆知的是学生常常对老师的批改一扫而过,去寻找最后的成绩。本书反其道而行之,把阅读和写作都作为学生与文本进行有意义的互动的过程,且过程和成果并重:不仅专注于学生的作品,而且更重要的,专注于这个作品的产生过程。

本着注重过程的宗旨,本书强调在阅读和写作中提高学生表达思想和结构文章的能力。外语学生往往忽略文章的内容:把阅读仅当作译解文本,而在写作时则只专注于改正语言的错误。教导学生同时注意过程和成果及为了全局的意义而不仅是局部的语言问题而修改写作是至关重要的。因此，本书的每一课包括一篇精读课文和四篇泛读课文。

- **写作指导**提出任务，讨论某种特定的体裁的结构、惯用法及风格特征。它提供帮助读者和作者深入字里行间的高定位的探询策略，诸如分析、综合及评估。在必要时，它也教学生通过时间顺序、因果关系或理由和证据的修辞模式构思，使读者和作者认识并应用思维策略。
- **范文**揭示某种特定体裁的结构、修辞和语言特征。每篇范文都是作者为本书量身定制的，学生读来会饶有兴趣因为它们和学生的生活经验是息息相通的。范文的特色是位于右边空白处的点评。这些点评帮助学生理解课文如何组织结构、思想如何关联、以及句子和段落如何扣题。有了这些点评，阅读进程就会特别活跃。
- **点评**分析范文，评估它的有效性、连贯性及语言的准确度和表达力。它阐明范文如何通过有趣的内容、独特的风格、有效的用词及多变的句型来保持读者的注意力。
- **修辞**突出范文中特殊的文学手段以便学生在自己的写作中运用自如。这七课包括以下的修辞手段：拟人、比喻、排比、夸张、联想、想象和设问。

此外，每课还有一篇**应用文**。这篇补充的泛读课文使学生有机会练习实用写作。这七课提供以下应用文的写作指导：电子邮件、祝词、感谢信、海报、求职信、简历和读后感。

本书的练习也相应地运用过程渐进方法设计，引导学生经历一个步步为营的写作训练。练习由三部分组成：词汇训练、语句训练和作文训练。这些训练不但为学生提供语料以填补他们的作文中的词语空挡，而且也帮助学生学会行文的诀窍。在第三部分，即作文训练中，各种作业都是富有创造性而又循序渐进的，包括仿写作文、情景作文、串联作文、进阶作文和应用文写作。

- **仿写作文**使学生能基于范文的写作技巧高效地写作。学生既可撰写新作，也可模仿作者的技巧修改旧文。学习作者的修辞结构、语法形态、过渡词语和使用重复、排比和归纳等写作技巧能促进理解和交流。
- **情景作文**教学生根据一个描绘清楚的情景有效地构想并组织文字。这需要具备对任务目的以及情景和读者的清醒了解。要仔细演绎、充分发挥并善于组织提示中的各项要点。
- **串联作文**是一种利用电子媒介做的文字游戏。学生每人写一个句子，联手创作一个逻辑性强又趣味盎然的故事。学生练习集体构思、发展和修改文章。学生也建立起作者与读者以及社团的感觉，并在课堂上发展这种绝妙的期待心理：我写文章并不只是完成老师的作业，也是为了给我的伙伴阅读。
- **进阶作文**是一个别出心裁的、循序渐进又环环相扣的系列习作，其目的是帮助学生写长写深。许多学生茫然不知如何填满一至两页的纸张。这项练习会引导学生一步一个台阶地前进，先写作为文章有机组成部分的段落，再把它们联结成为浑然一体的作文。

这个着眼于体裁、注重于过程的高级中文阅读写作教学法是教学经验的积累，也是经实践证明的、生动有趣又容易实施的。本书说明无论是学生或老师都无须对阅读和写作望而生畏。构思、起草和修改文章对学生领悟阅读材料的内容、结构、发展和风格的作用至巨。因此，他们的阅读会由"解码"状态转为积极的解读，他们的写作会逐渐地与口语分道扬镳，增强句法的深度和词汇的难度。总之，本书阅读与写作结合的策略，使老师和学生能收 "一石二鸟" 之功效。

User's guide 使用说明

1 This book can be used as the textbook for a special course of reading and writing, but it is primarily designed as the main textbook of an advanced (third or fourth year in college) Chinese course.

2 There are five texts in each lesson: "Writing Guide," "Model Text," "Commentary," "Rhetoric," and "Practical Writing," as well as five vocabulary lists. Among them, "Model Text" is the text for "intensive reading" 精读. As far as the other four texts are concerned, the instructor may use them as "extensive reading" 泛读 based on the students' levels.

3 The amount of exercises can be adjusted according to teachers' preferences in order to maintain an adequate workload for students.

4 English translations follow the four "extensive reading" texts in order to help students accelerate their reading speed. The English translations of the Model Texts, however, are provided in the Appendices.

使用说明

1　本书可作为专门读写课程的教材，但主要是设计为高年级中文课程（大学三年级或四年级）的主要教材。
2　每课有五篇课文：《写作指导》、《范文》、《点评》、《修辞》和《应用文》及五个词汇表。其中，《范文》是精读课文。至于其它的四篇，老师可根据学生的水平，把它们作为泛读课文。
3　教师可根据自己的意愿调整练习的数量以保持适当程度的学生工作量。
4　四篇泛读课文的英文翻译紧随其后以帮助学生加快阅读速度，但范文的英译收在附录中。

1 第一课　Writing about events, part one
记事篇上

1.1 Writing guide 写作指导

Key elements of event writing 记事要素

记叙文有六个要素：时间、地点、人物、事件的起因、经过和结果。

一个事件总是在一定的时段中发生、发展和变化。比如，上午、下午、晚上是一天的时段；上课前、上课时、下课后是一节课的时段；童年、少年、青年是人生的时段。以时间为序，组织材料，叫顺叙。用顺叙的法子，可以把事件的起因、经过和结果交代得很清楚。有时也可用倒叙，使文章结构富于变化，造成悬念，引人入胜。

不管用哪种法子，文笔一定要生动。此外，要通过对事件的叙述和描写，直接或间接地表达作者的思想。

Narratives have six key elements: time, place, character, as well as an event's cause, progression, and result.

An event always occurs, develops, and changes within a certain time frame. For example, morning, afternoon, and night are time periods within a day; before class begins, during class, and after class ends are class time periods; childhood, adolescence, and young adulthood are stages of life. Organizing material in order of the time of occurrence is called narrating in chronological order. By implementing this method of recounting events in chronological order, it's possible to account for cause, progression, and result very clearly. Sometimes one may also use flashback, which makes a composition even richer in structural change in addition to causing suspense and leading the reader to find the piece more interesting.

Regardless of which type of method is used, the style of writing must be lively. Furthermore, through the narration and description of an event, one must express the author's thoughts directly or indirectly.

词汇一

1	指导	指導	zhǐdǎo	instruction, guide
2	记叙文	記敘文	jìxùwén	narrative
3	要素		yàosù	key element
4	事件		shìjiàn	event, incident
5	起因		qǐyīn	cause, reason
6	经过	經過	jīngguò	process, course
7	时段	時段	shíduàn	period of time
8	以...为序	以...爲序	yǐ...wéixù	in order of
9	组织	組織	zǔzhī	to organize, arrange
10	材料		cáiliào	material

11	顺叙	順敘	shùnxù	to narrate in chronological order
12	交代		jiāodài	to tell, account for
13	倒叙	倒敘	dàoxù	flashback
14	结构	結構	jiégòu	structure, composition
15	富于		fùyú	to be rich in, be full of
16	悬念	懸念	xuánniàn	suspense
17	引人入胜	引人入勝	yǐnrénrùshèng	to lead one into the interesting part of something, alluring, fascinating
18	文笔	文筆	wénbǐ	style of writing
19	叙述	敘述	xùshù	to narrate, give an account of
20	直接		zhíjiē	direct
21	间接	間接	jiànjiē	indirect

1.2 Model text 范文

An amusing account of exam preparations 备考趣记

【提示】古人有 "悬梁刺股" 等开夜车的办法。你们都 "身经百战" – 经过无数次的考试，一定有不少开夜车的经历与办法。写一个真实的故事，一定要有趣。

Ancient people had a variety of methods that aided them in working through the night, such as "tying one's hair to the house beam and poking one's thigh with an awl." You are all "veterans"– you have been through countless tests, certainly you have much experience and know many methods for keeping yourself awake while studying late into the night. Write an interesting story of these accounts.

明天是商业法课的期终考试。这是我最怕的一门课，要死记硬背很多法律条文。没办法，我今晚就住在图书馆里，通宵备考了。

- 人物1：我
- 事件起因：准备商业法考试
- 时间：晚上
- 地点：图书馆

晚上十一点，我精神抖擞地走进图书馆，找了个安静的角落，在沙发上坐下。我从书包中掏出两罐 "红牛"，立在前面的矮桌上，像两个斗志昂扬的战士，守护着我的时间。古人开夜车要 "悬梁刺股"，现代学子可不必受这份罪了。

- 串联物红牛1
- 人物2：劳拉

刚打开砖头一般的课本，口袋里的苹果手机就开始振动了。一看，是死党劳拉发来的短信："你在哪里?"我想，两人一起复习也好，可以一问一答，帮助记忆。

劳拉一坐下，就跟我抱怨今天下午的中文考试。在回答题目 "你的志愿" 时，她本要写 "大使"。可是一不小心，把 "使" 字写成了 "便" 字。我一听，经不住狂笑起来。等我俩把中文考试中的错误互相讥笑了一遍，已经午夜了。

- 事件发展1：讨论中文题

我们马上开始问答。劳拉刚问我："第一个破产法是在哪里制定的？" 忽然听到有人叫："在这里!"一看，原来是我的另外两个死党琳达和丽莎来了。两人一坐下，就说考完试，一定要去哪儿玩个痛快。于是四人开始讨论旅游计划。到最后决定去佛罗里达坐豪华游轮，已经两点了，肚子开始提抗议了。琳达说："腹中空空怎么能复习呢？咱们去珍珠奶茶店吃夜宵吧！"

- 人物3、4：琳达、丽莎
- 事件发展2：讨论旅游
- 事件发展3：吃夜宵

吃了夜宵回来，时针指着三点。商业法实在太没劲，刚问答了几条，大家的上下眼皮开始打架了。看着两个空的红牛罐头子东倒西歪地躺在桌子上，丽莎说："现在你再喝十罐红牛也没用。现在肚子饱了，脑子空了。不如打个盹儿，头脑清醒了再复习。"此话有理，大家就在沙发上横躺下来。

只听劳拉大叫一声："不好了！七点半了！"大家吓得连忙跳起来，把书往书包里一塞，把红牛罐头子扔进垃圾箱，就往教室奔去。八点钟要考商业法呢。

- 串联物红牛2
- 事件发展4：打盹儿

- 串联物红牛3
- 结局：没有备考

词汇二

1	范文	範文	fànwén	model essay
2	备考	備考	bèikǎo	准备考试
3	提示		tíshì	guide, cue
4	悬	懸	xuán	挂, to hang
5	梁		liáng	beam
6	刺		cì	to stab, prick
7	股		gǔ	大腿, thigh
8	悬梁刺股	懸梁刺股	xuánliáng cìgǔ	tying one's hair to the house beam and poking one's thigh with an awl to keep oneself awake – painstaking in one's study (See Note 1)
9	开夜车	開夜車	kāiyèchē	to work late into the night
10	身经百战	身經百戰	shēnjīng bǎizhàn	to be a veteran in battle, be battle-seasoned
11	无数	無數	wúshù	innumerable, countless
12	经历	經歷	jīnglì	experience
13	真实	真實	zhēnshí	real, true
14	法		fǎ	法律, law
15	期终	期終	qīzhōng	end of the semester
16	死记硬背	死記硬背	sǐjì yìngbèi	mechanical memorizing
17	条文	條文	tiáowén	article, clause
18	通宵		tōngxiāo	all night, throughout the night
19	精神抖擞	精神抖擻	jīngshén dǒusǒu	vigorous, energetic
20	角落		jiǎoluò	corner
21	掏		tāo	to take out, draw out
22	罐		guàn	jar, can
23	红牛	紅牛	hóngniú	Red Bull (an energy drink)
24	斗志昂扬	鬥志昂揚	dòuzhì ángyáng	to have a strong fighting spirit, have high morale
25	守护	守護	shǒuhù	to guard, protect
26	串联	串聯	chuànlián	to connect or make a series
27	学子	學子	xuézǐ	学生
28	受罪		shòuzuì	to suffer
29	砖头	磚頭	zhuāntóu	brick
30	一般		yībān	一样
31	口袋		kǒudài	pocket
32	振动	振動	zhèndòng	to vibrate
33	党	黨	dǎng	party
34	死党	死黨	sǐdǎng	diehard followers, best friends
35	劳拉	勞拉	láolā	Laura

36	发	發	fā	to send, deliver
37	短信		duǎnxìn	short message
38	记忆	記憶	jìyì	memorization
39	抱怨		bàoyuàn	to complain
40	志愿	志願	zhìyuàn	aspiration, wish
41	本		běn	原来, originally
42	一不小心		yībù xiǎoxīn	with a reckless negligence
43	经不住	經不住	jīngbùzhù	cannot withhold, must
44	狂		kuáng	wild, violent
45	讥笑	譏笑	jīxiào	to ridicule
46	午夜		wǔyè	midnight
47	破产	破產	pòchǎn	bankruptcy
48	制定		zhìdìng	to constitute, establish
49	琳达	琳達	líndá	Linda
50	丽莎	麗莎	lìshā	Lisa
51	痛快		tòngkuài	to one's great satisfaction
52	佛罗里达	佛羅裏達	fúluólǐdá	Florida
53	豪华	豪華	háohuá	luxurious
54	豪华游轮	豪華遊輪	háohuá yóulún	cruise
55	抗议	抗議	kàngyì	to protest
56	腹		fù	abdomen, belly
57	珍珠		zhēnzhū	pearl
58	珍珠奶茶		zhēnzhū nǎichá	bubble tea
59	夜宵		yèxiāo	midnight snack
60	时针	時針	shízhēn	hour hand
61	实在	實在	shízài	really
62	没劲	沒勁	méijìn	boring
63	眼皮		yǎnpí	eyelids
64	打架		dǎjià	to fight
65	东倒西歪	東倒西歪	dōngdǎo xīwāi	to waver east and west, fall over like ninepins
66	打盹儿	打盹兒	dǎdǔnr	to doze off, take a nap
67	头脑	頭腦	tóunǎo	brain; mind
68	清醒		qīngxǐng	sober, clear-headed
69	此		cǐ	this
70	有理		yǒulǐ	reasonable, justified
71	横	橫	héng	horizontal, transverse
72	吓	嚇	xià	to scare, frighten
73	连忙	連忙	liánmáng	hastily, promptly
74	塞		sāi	to stuff, squeeze in
75	垃圾		lājī	garbage, litter

Note 1: 悬梁刺股 (tying one's hair to the house beam and poking one's thigh with an awl). This proverb is composed of two historical stories that illustrate unique ways of keeping oneself awake while studying hard into late night. Sun Jing 孙敬 of the Eastern Han Dynasty (25–220) tied his hair to one end of a string and tied the other end of the string to the beams of his house. Therefore, whenever he dozed off, his hair would be pulled and he would wake up. Su Qin 苏秦 of the Warring States period (475–221 BCE) implemented a different method to keep himself awake. Whenever he felt tired, he would poke his thigh with an awl and the sharp pain would arouse him. As a result of their painstaking studies, both of these scholars had outstanding careers.

1.3 Commentary 点评

这篇短文写得很有生活气息，也非常有趣。学生读了都笑了，因为很多人有过类似的经历。

　　文章用顺叙的法子，故事随着时间发展，读来觉得结构紧凑、层次清楚。

　　除了时间，这个故事另外还成功地运用了一条线索，那就是红牛。红牛一开始是作者的法宝，后来逐渐失效，最后被扔进垃圾箱。这条线索跟故事并行发展，起了很好的串联作用。

　　作者叙述的是她的一次失败的经历，并没有讲道理。但实际上主题思想是很清楚的：备考不能靠红牛，要靠自己抓紧时间。

This short essay is infused with life, and it's also very interesting. All students laugh upon reading it, because many of them have similar experiences.

The essay uses chronological narrative methods. As time goes on and the story develops, it appears that the structure is very organized and the materials are well-arranged.

Aside from time, this story also succeeds in implementing a thread, which is the Red Bull. Red Bull begins as the author's talisman, which later on gradually loses its effectiveness, and finally it's tossed away into the garbage bin. This thread develops along with the story as a function of connecting a series of events.

What the author recounts is her experience of failure, and it may seem that the story does not teach a lesson. However, the theme is actually very clear: While preparing for a test, you can't rely on Red Bull; instead, you must rely on your own ability to manage your time.

词汇三

1	点评	點評	diǎnpíng	critique, commentary
2	气息	氣息	qìxī	tinge, atmosphere
3	类似	類似	lèisì	similar
4	紧凑	緊湊	jǐncòu	tight, well-knit, well-organized sequence of ideas (in writing or speech)
5	层次	層次	céngcì	level
6	线索	線索	xiànsuǒ	clue, thread
7	法宝	法寶	fǎbǎo	talisman, trump
8	逐渐	逐漸	zhújiàn	gradually
9	失效		shīxiào	to expire, lose effectiveness
10	并行	並行	bìngxíng	parallel, to go side by side
11	起作用		qǐ zuòyòng	to play a part
12	失败	失敗	shībài	to be defeated, failure
13	主题		zhǔtí	theme, motif
14	主题思想		zhǔtí sīxiǎng	main idea
15	抓紧	抓緊	zhuājǐn	to keep a firm grasp on, pay close attention to

1.4 Rhetoric 修辞

Personification 拟人

拟人就是根据想象把物当作人来叙述或描写，使物具有人一样的言行、神态、思想和感情。比如："星星眨着眼睛"、"风翻开了书"、"花儿随风舞蹈"、"行道树笔直地站在路边"等等。

《备考趣记》也用了不少拟人句，比如：红牛 "像两个斗志昂扬的战士，守护着我的时间"、"肚子开始提抗议了"、"大家的上下眼皮开始打架了"、"两个空的红牛罐头东倒西歪地躺在桌子上"。用写人的词句去写物，往往能比较形象、生动。

Personification involves using imagination to take things and treat them like people with respect to narration and description. It characterizes things as possessing human-like speechs, actions, manners, thoughts, and feelings. For example: "The stars blink," "the wind turns over the book," "the flowers dance in the wind," "the trees stand upright along the side of the road," etc.

"An Amusing Account of Exam Preparations" also uses personification in many sentences. For example: Red Bull is "like two soldiers with a strong fighting spirit, safeguarding my time," "my stomach began to protest," "everyone's drooping eyelids fought to stay open," and "two empty Red Bull cans lay scattered on the table." By using words attributed to people to write about objects, it will more often than not provide a relatively vivid and lively image.

词汇四

1	修辞	修辭	xiūcí	rhetoric
2	拟人	擬人	nǐrén	personification
3	根据	根據	gēnjù	on the basis of, according to
4	物		wù	thing, object
5	当做	當做	dàngzuò	to treat as, regard as
6	具有		jùyǒu	to possess, have
7	言行		yánxíng	words and deeds, speech and action
8	神态	神態	shéntài	expression, manner, bearing
9	眨		zhǎ	to blink, wink
10	翻		fān	to turn (over, up, inside out, etc.)
11	行道树	行道樹	xíngdào shù	roadside or sidewalk trees
12	笔直	筆直	bǐzhí	perfectly straight; bolt upright
13	形象		xíngxiàng	image, figure

1.5 Practical writing 应用文

Email 电子邮件

对现在的大学生来说，写信可能已经是一种历史知识了。他们是成长在电子邮件的时代。写电子邮件比写信要方便得多，也更随便，但还是有一些基本规则要注意的。

由于在电脑屏幕和手机上阅读跟在纸上阅读有所不同，电子邮件的结构和格式也有不同。段落要短，段落之间一般要有空行。如果有几个并列的要点，可把它们并行排列，编号或用重点号。

邮件不要太长，句子也要简明扼要。如果一个人收到一个很长的电子邮件，有可能他就不想读了。

每封电子邮件都要有个标题。标题要很清楚地反映邮件的内容。这样，方便收件人，也便于搜索。

电子邮件跟电话、信件的一个不同之处就是比较随便，因此可以省略一些寒暄语，直接进入主题。

最后，写电子邮件图的是快捷，但在点击"发送"键之前，要看清楚发送地址，可别送错了邮箱！

As far as today's college students are concerned, writing letters may already be considered a type of historical knowledge. They have grown up in the email age. Writing an email is much more convenient than writing a letter and it's also more casual, but it still has some basic rules that one must abide by.

Since reading on a computer screen and a cellphone is somewhat different than reading from a piece of paper, an email's composition and format is also different. Paragraphs need to be short, and between paragraphs, there is usually a space. If there are a few juxtaposing key points, one could arrange them in parallel, number them, or use bullet points to separate them.

Emails don't need to be very long, and sentences should also be concise. If a person receives a very long email, it may be possible that he or she will not want to read it.

Every email must have a subject line. The subject should clearly reflect the email's content. Thus, it's convenient for the recipient, and it's also easier to search for.

Emails, when compared to phone calls and letters, are different in that they are relatively casual, so one can omit conventional greetings and skip directly to the subject of the email.

Lastly, writing an email is quick, but before clicking the "send" key, one must look clearly at the email's destination, so one would not accidentally send it to the wrong inbox!

词汇五

1	应用	應用	yìngyòng	to use, apply
2	应用文	應用文	yìngyòngwén	practical writing
3	对...来说	對...來說	duì...láishuō	to, regarding
4	成长	成長	chéngzhǎng	to grow up
5	基本		jīběn	basic, essential
6	规则	規則	guīzé	rule, regulation
7	屏幕		píngmù	screen
8	格式		géshì	format, layout
9	段落		duànluò	paragraph
10	之间	之間	zhījiān	between, among
11	行		háng	line, row
12	并列	並列	bìngliè	to juxtapose
13	要点	要點	yàodiǎn	key point, essentials
14	排列	排列	páiliè	to arrange, put in order
15	编号	編號	biānhào	to number
16	重点号	重點號	zhòngdiǎn hào	emphasis mark, bullet
17	重点	重點	zhòngdiǎn	key point, emphasis
18	号	號	hào	mark, sign
19	简明	簡明	jiǎnmíng	concise, simple, and clear
20	扼要		èyào	concise, to the point, brief, and precise
21	标题	標題	biāotí	title, heading
22	反映		fǎnyìng	to reflect
23	内容	內容	nèiróng	content, substance
24	收件人		shōujiàn rén	receiver, consignee
25	便于		biànyú	to be easy to, convenient for
26	搜索		sōusuǒ	to search
27	省略		shěnglüè	to omit, skip
28	寒暄		hánxuān	exchange of conventional greetings
29	寒暄语	寒暄語	hánxuānyǔ	pleasantries
30	图	圖	tú	to pursue, seek
31	快捷		kuàijié	quick, speedy
32	点击	點擊	diǎnjī	to click (a computer mouse button)
33	击	擊	jī	to hit, beat
34	发送	發送	fāsòng	to send, transmit
35	键	鍵	jiàn	key (on a computer keyboard)

1.6 **Vocabulary training** 词汇训练

一、填名词 Fill in the blanks with appropriate nouns to form adjective-noun phrases.

1 清楚的 ____
2 生动的 ____
3 直接的 ____
4 间接的 ____
5 真实的 ____
6 安静的 ____
7 豪华的 ____
8 清醒的 ____
9 有趣的 ____
10 紧凑的 ____
11 失败的 ____
12 想像的 ____
13 笔直的 ____
14 方便的 ____
15 随便的 ____
16 并列的 ____
17 简明的 ____
18 扼要的 ____
19 准确的 ____

二、选词填空 Fill in the blanks correctly with the words provided.

1 一个事件总是在一定的 ____ 中发生、发展、变化。

   a. 时代   c. 时候
   b. 时段   d. 时光

2 用顺叙的法子，可以把事件的起因、经过和结果交代得很 ____ 。

   a. 清洁   c. 清楚
   b. 清静   d. 清高

3 商业法课是我最怕的一门课，要死记硬背很多法律 ____ 。

   a. 条文   c. 作文
   b. 课文   d. 公文

4 刚打开砖头一般的课本，口袋里的苹果开始 ____ 了。

   a. 激动   c. 活动
   b. 走动   d. 振动

5 等咱俩把中文考试中的错误互相 ____ 了一遍，已经午夜了。

   a. 欢笑   c. 讥笑
   b. 苦笑   d. 玩笑

6 劳拉问我：“第一个破产法是在哪里 ____ 的？”

   a. 决定   c. 确定
   b. 制定   d. 指定

7 两人一坐下，就说考完试，一定要去哪儿玩个 ____ 。

    a. 愉快   c. 飞快
    b. 欢快   d. 痛快

8 已经是两点了，肚子开始提 ____ 了。

    a. 建议   c. 商议
    b. 抗议   d. 争议

9 这篇短文写得很有生活 ____ 。

    a. 气味   c. 气候
    b. 气氛   d. 气息

10 对现在的大学生来说，写信可能已是一种历史 ____ 了。

    a. 常识   c. 认识
    b. 知识   d. 学识

11 写电子邮件比写信要方便得多，但还是有一些基本 ____ 要注意的。

    a. 规则   c. 方法
    b. 原理   d. 特点

12 邮件不要太长，句子也要简明 ____ 。

    a. 扼要   c. 重要
    b. 主要   d. 必要

13 每封电子邮件都要有个 ____ 。

    a. 主题   c. 标题
    b. 问题   d. 课题

14 标题要很 ____ 地反映邮件的内容。

    a. 充分   c. 有趣
    b. 清楚   d. 准确

15 在点击 ____ 键之前，要看清楚发送地址，可别送错了邮箱！

    a. 退出   c. 删除
    b. 储存   d. 发送

三、改错 Correct the errors.

1 用倒叙的法子，可以把事件的起因、经过和结果交代得很清楚。
2 我从书包中掏出两罐黑莓，立在前面的矮桌上。
3 到最后决定去阿拉斯加坐豪华游轮，已经是两点了。
4 刚问答了几条，大家的上下眼皮开始吵架了。
5 大家吓得连忙跳起来，把红牛罐子头往书包里一塞，就往教室奔去。
6 作者叙述的是她的一次成功的经历，并没有讲道理。
7 实际上主题思想是很清楚的：备考要靠红牛。
8 拟人就是根据想象把人当作物来叙述或描写。
9 电子邮件的标题要很准确地反映邮件的内容。这样，方便写信人。
10 写电子邮件可以省略一些寒暄语，直接进入标题。

1.7 Phrase training 语句训练

一、用句型造句 Make sentences using the following sentence patterns.

1　不管......一定

【课文例句】不管用哪种法子，文笔一定要生动。
【生活例句】妈，不管你同意不同意，我一定要去纽约看我的朋友，我们已经一年没见面了。

Mom, no matter whether you agree or disagree, I must go to New York to see my friend. We haven't seen each other for a year.

2　刚......就

【课文例句】刚打开砖头一般的课本，口袋里的苹果手机就开始振动了。
【生活例句】他们俩刚结婚了半年，怎么就要离婚了呢？

Those two were only married for half a year, how can they already want a divorce?

3　一......就

【课文例句】劳拉一坐下，就跟我抱怨今天下午的中文考试。
【生活例句】张经理一走进办公室，所有的人就都停止了讲话。大家都怕他。

As soon as Manager Zhang stepped into the office, everyone immediately stopped talking. Everyone feared him.

4　等（到）......已经

【课文例句】等咱俩把中文考试中的错误互相讥笑了一遍，已经午夜了。
【生活例句】刘文华老是迟到，今天等他来到饭店，我们已经把菜都吃完了，就剩下一大碗饭给他。

Liu Wenhua is always late. Today when he arrived at the restaurant, we had already finished all the dishes, only leaving him a big bowl of rice.

5　刚......忽然

【课文例句】劳拉刚问我："第一个破产法是在哪里制定的？""忽然听到有人叫："在这里！"
【生活例句】李明刚进机场大门，忽然想到他把护照留在家里了。

Li Ming had just entered the front gate of the airport when suddenly he realized he had left his passport at home.

6　刚......开始

【课文例句】刚问答了几条，大家的上下眼皮开始打架了。
【生活例句】他刚上班，怎么就开始对公司不满意了呢？

He just started working. How come he has already begun to feel unsatisfied with the company?

7　现在......不如

【课文例句】现在肚子饱了，脑子空了。不如打个盹儿，头脑清醒了再复习。
【生活例句】现在看八点的电影已经晚了，不如看十点的吧。

Now it's already too late to see the 8 o'clock movie. It's better to see the 10 o'clock movie instead.

8　很⋯⋯也

【课文例句】这篇短文写得很有生活气息，也非常有趣。
【生活例句】赵万山参加很多课外活动，他不但是校刊编辑，也是篮球队长。

Zhao Wanshan participates in many extracurricular activities. He's not only the university magazine's editor, but he's also the basketball team's captain.

9　除了⋯⋯还

【课文例句】除了时间，这个故事另外还成功地运用了一条线索。
【生活例句】李勇很注意身体健康，他每天除了去健身房锻炼，还去游泳馆游泳。

Li Yong pays much attention to his health. Not only does he go to the gym to exercise every day, he also goes to the swimming pool to swim.

10　起了⋯⋯作用

【课文例句】这条线索跟故事并行发展，起了很好的串联作用。
【生活例句】陈天云每个星期抽时间帮助一个中学生，对她成功进入一个好大学起了很大的作用。

Chen Tianyun put aside time to help a high school student every week, which played an important role for the student to get into a good college.

11　一开始⋯⋯后来⋯⋯最后

【课文例句】红牛一开始是作者的法宝，后来逐渐失效，最后被扔进垃圾箱。
【生活例句】高一的时候大家觉得王青云不怎么聪明，后来她一个个考试越考越好，最后毕业时成绩全班第一。

During freshman year of high school, everyone thought Wang Qingyun wasn't very smart, but later she did better and better on tests, and finally she became first in her class by graduation.

12　把⋯⋯当做

【课文例句】拟人就是根据想象把物当做人来叙述或描写。
【生活例句】小花的妈妈看起来特别年轻，很多人把她当做小花的姐姐了。

Xiaohua's mother looks especially young, and many people think that she is Xiaohua's older sister.

13　对⋯⋯来说

【课文例句】对现在的大学生来说，写信可能已是一种历史知识了。
【生活例句】对一些穷人的孩子来说，去迪士尼乐园玩是一个美丽的梦想。

For some destitute children, going to Disneyland is a beautiful dream.

14　如果⋯⋯有可能

【课文例句】如果一个人收到一个很长的电子邮件，有可能他就不想读了。
【生活例句】如果我被清华大学录取了，我就有可能不去牛津大学留学了。

If I'm admitted into Tsinghua University, there's a chance that I won't go to study at Oxford University.

二、回答问题 Answer the questions.

1 记事的文章有哪 六个要素？
2 什么叫顺叙？用顺叙的法子有什么好处？
3 为什么 "我" 最怕商业法课？
4 为什么 "我" 今晚要住在图书馆里？
5 两人一起复习有什么好处？
6 劳拉在中文考试中犯了什么错误？
7 为什么吃了夜宵回来大家的上下眼皮开始打架了？
8 为什么学生看了这篇文章都笑了？
9 红牛在故事中起了什么作用？请说明。
10 这个故事的主题思想是什么？
11 本文哪些地方写得很生动？请你举一个例子并加以分析说明。
12 本文哪些句子写得很有趣？请你举一个例子并加以分析说明。
13 列出 "我" 准备考试的时间表，说明本文叙述的顺序。
14 说明记事的六要素在本文中的体现。
15 写一个你在以前的中文考试中犯的比较好笑的错误。
16 什么是拟人？
17 电子邮件和信的结构和格式有什么不同？

三、选词填空，运用拟人手法完成句子 Fill in the blanks with a word chosen from the parentheses to complete the sentences using personification:

1 小树被大风吹弯了 ____ 。(背、腰)
2 小鸟在树上欢快地 ____ 。（歌唱、舞蹈）
3 树上的苹果向我们点 ____ 微笑。（头、手）
4 村边的小河静静地 ____ 在大地的怀抱里。（坐、躺）

1.8 Composition training 作文训练

一、仿写作文 *Imitative composition*

写一个题为《备考趣记》的故事，要符合以下三个要求：1. 用第一人称写；2. 要用上记事的六个要素；3. 用上拟人的手法。故事的长度不限。

Write a story titled "An Amusing Account of Exam Preparations" 备考趣记 following these three requirements: 1. Write in the first person. 2. Include the six major elements of the narrative. 3. Use personification. The length of the story is flexible.

二、情景作文 *Situational composition*

结合范文中的情景，补写一段四位姑娘讨论旅游计划的文字，要包括叙述和对话。

Referring to the Model Text, write a paragraph of the four girls discussing their travel plans. Include both a narrative and a conversation.

三、串联作文 *Chain story composition*

这个练习是全班同学作为课外作业的集体创作。根据姓名的英文字母的排列，每人依次写一句。故事会放在 "黑板" 或其他类似的课堂教学管理系统的讨论板上。故事的开端提供在下面。尽量使故事易懂、逻辑性强和生动有趣。尽可能多用拟人句。你一看到你前面的同学写好了，就应着手写作。一圈下来，轮到的任何人只要觉得故事应该到此为止，就可以结束故事。此后，班上要举行一次讨论。

This will be a collective story created by the whole class as homework. According to the alphabetical order of the class list, each writer is succeeded by the next student. The story will be posted on the discussion board on Blackboard© or a similar learning management system. The beginning of the story is provided below. Try to make the story understandable, logical and interesting. Use personification to the best of your ability. You should begin to write your sentence as soon as you see that the preceding one is completed. After the first round, anybody during his or her turn can conclude the story if he or she thinks it is right place to do so. A class discussion of the story will follow.

题目：《惊喜聚会》

"叮铃铃⋯⋯"一阵电话铃把我吵醒了。嗨，谁这么讨厌，星期天上午还不让人睡个懒觉啊？⋯⋯

四、进阶作文 *Sequential composition*

以《我的手机》为题，写三篇短文。

Write three short pieces in sequence with the title of "My Cellphone."

1 写一个100字左右的段落，描写你的手机：它的形状、色彩、功能等。

Write a paragraph of about 100 characters, describing your cellphone's shape, color, features, etc.

2 写两个100字左右的段落，记叙你的手机的历史：你是怎么得到它的？用了多久？发生过什么有意思的事吗？

Write a short piece with two 100-character paragraphs, telling the history of your cellphone: Where did you get it? How long have you been using it? Are there any interesting stories about your cellphone?

3 结合上述的三个段落的内容，写一个500字的小故事。要包括记事的六个要素。

Combine the contents of the three aforementioned paragraphs, and write a story of about 500 characters. It should include the six elements of event writing.

五、应用文写作 *Practical composition*

给班上的一个同学发一个电子邮件，请求一个帮助。你收到同学的邮件后要回复，并适当的回应他的要求。

Send an email to a classmate, and make a request. Also, respond to the email from your classmate and answer his or her request appropriately.

2 第二课 Writing about events, part two
记事篇下

2.1 Writing guide 写作指导

Detailed descriptions 细节描写

一篇记事文，有了好的结构，还要注意细节描写。中国古代哲学家老子说过："天下大事，必作于细。"做事要注意细节，写文章也要注意细节。

如果你写道："刚进大学，我很想家，就打电话回家，我说，妈妈我想你，妈妈说她也想我......"只见概述不见描写，更不见细节，就显得语言枯燥，人物形象模糊，感情平淡。

细节描写是指对人物的细微的行动和故事的细小的情节作具体细腻的描写。这些细节往往能对刻画人物形象、发展故事情节以及深化文章主题起到很大的作用。

When writing a narrative piece with good structure, the author also needs to pay close attention to the description of details. The ancient Chinese philosopher Laozi said: "The great things under heaven must start from smaller components." When doing anything, it's necessary to pay attention to detail, and so when writing an article, you must also pay attention to detail.

If you wrote: "When I first entered college, I missed my family very much. So I called home and said, 'Mom I miss you;' and my mother said, 'I also miss you. . . .'" there is only a summary of the encounter and no descriptions, let alone details. Therefore, the language appears boring, the images of the characters are unclear, and the feelings conveyed are dulled.

Detailed descriptions refer to exquisite descriptions of characters' subtle actions and the story's fine plot points. These details more often than not play a large role in painting an image of the characters, developing the plot, as well as enriching the article's theme.

词汇一

1	细	細	xì	小
2	细节	細節	xìjié	detail
3	哲学家	哲學家	zhéxuéjiā	philosopher
4	老子		lǎozǐ	Laozi, founder of Daoism
5	天下		tiānxià	land under heaven, world
6	必		bì	一定, must
7	概述		gàishù	outline, summary
8	显得	顯得	xiǎnde	to seem, look, appear
9	枯燥		kūzào	dull and dry, uninteresting
10	模糊		móhu	不清楚, vague, indistinct

11	感情		gǎnqíng	emotion, feeling, affection
12	平淡		píngdàn	dull, uninteresting
13	细微	細微	xìwēi	subtle, slight
14	情节	情節	qíngjié	plot, details of a story
15	具体	具體	jùtǐ	concrete, specific
16	细腻	細腻	xìnì	delicate, exquisite
17	刻画	刻畫	kèhuà	to depict, portray
18	深化		shēnhuà	to deepen, reinforce

2.2 Model text 范文

A tune in the rain 雨中曲

【提示】有个美国音乐剧叫*Singin' in the Rain* ，中文译名叫 "雨中曲"。我们借用这个名字写一篇作文。这个 "曲" 字，在这儿不一定是 "乐曲" 的曲，也可以是 "插曲" 的曲：写一件在下雨天发生的事。注意细节描写。

There's an American musical called *Singin' in the Rain*, and the Chinese translation of this name is "A Tune in the Rain." We have borrowed this name for the title of our piece. This *qu*曲 character, is not necessarily the *qu*曲 of *yuequ*乐曲(music), but it can also be read as the *qu*曲 of *chaqu*插曲(episode). Write about what occurs in the rain and pay close attention to detail.

中文课上，老师说明天要表演小品，并指定我和马克一起准备。下课时，我们匆匆约好了晚上八点一起排练，也没来得及说地点。

- 事件起因

谁知，吃好晚饭刚回到宿舍，突然窗外狂风大作，天上乌云翻滚。随着一道道闪电和一阵阵雷声，豆大的雨点从天空中落下来，像鞭子一样抽打着窗户。

- 细节1：窗外雨景

我给马克打电话，想问他我们在哪儿见面，可是手机没信号了。这个鬼天气！眼看七点三刻了，同屋的汤姆指着窗外说："你看，外边的路都成了黄河长江了，你何必出去呢？马克也肯定呆在家里看电视了。" 我说 "那我就去他宿舍吧。要是不排练，明天我们怎么表演呢？" 说罢，我鼓起勇气，拿把伞，冲出门去。

- 细节2：路上水流成河

- 事件发展：冒雨赴约

没走几步，一阵大风刮来，我的伞就吹了喇叭。好不容易把伞翻过来，人早就成了落汤鸡。电影《雨中曲》里，那个男演员拿着伞边跳边唱，成为传世经典。要是在这样的倾盆大雨中，料他也跳不起来了。

- 细节3：伞吹了喇叭

大风迎面刮来，我只能把伞撑在胸前，低着头往前走。不料，一脚踩在一个水坑里，人站不稳，就摔了下去。等我爬起来，已经沾了一脸的泥水，眼睛都看不清了。这时我的脸一定像京剧中的大花脸了。

- 细节4：泥水里摔跤

- 细节5：花脸

走到马克的宿舍，身上的水像小溪般直往下流，脚下立即积起了一滩水。我一边敲门，一边想：不管怎样，我们可以好好排练了。

- 细节6：脚下一滩水

一会儿，马克的同屋来开了门。一看是我，他满脸的疑惑："你怎么来了？马克去你的宿舍了！"

- 结局：出乎意外

词汇二

1	曲		qǔ	song, tune, melody
2	音乐剧	音樂劇	yīnyuèjù	musical
3	译名	譯名	yìmíng	translated name or term
4	借用		jièyòng	to borrow, take
5	乐曲	樂曲	yuèqǔ	musical composition
6	插曲		chāqǔ	episode, incident
7	表演		biǎoyǎn	to perform, act
8	小品		xiǎopǐn	skit
9	指定		zhǐdìng	to appoint, assign
10	马克	馬克	mǎkè	Mark
11	匆匆		cōngcōng	hastily, in a hurry
12	排练	排練	páiliàn	to rehearse
13	狂风大作	狂風大作	kuángfēng dàzuò	刮大风
14	乌云	烏雲	wūyún	dark clouds
15	翻滚	翻滾	fāngǔn	to roll, tumble
16	道		dào	a flash of
17	闪电	閃電	shǎndiàn	lightning
18	阵	陣	zhèn	*a measure word for a period of time*
19	雷		léi	thunder
20	豆		dòu	bean
21	雨点	雨點	yǔdiǎn	raindrop
22	鞭子		biānzi	whip, lash
23	抽打		chōudǎ	to strike, lash
24	信号	信號	xìnhào	signal
25	鬼		guǐ	terrible, nasty (weather, place, etc.)
26	眼看		yǎnkàn	soon, shortly
27	指		zhǐ	to point
28	何必		hébì	*used in rhetorical questions to indicate that there is no need to do something*
29	肯定		kěndìng	certainly, surely
30	呆		dāi	to stay
31	(说)罢	(說)罷	(shuō)bà	as soon as finished (talking)
32	鼓起勇气	鼓起勇氣	gǔqǐ yǒngqì	to pluck up one's courage
33	冲	衝	chōng	to charge, rush; dash
34	冒雨		màoyǔ	to brave rains
35	赴约	赴約	fùyuē	to go to an appointment
36	喇叭		lǎba	trumpet, horn
37	好不容易		hǎobùróngyì	with great difficulty
38	落汤鸡	落湯雞	luòtāng jī	like a chicken in soup, soaked through
39	传世	傳世	chuánshì	to be handed down from ancient times
40	经典	經典	jīngdiǎn	classics
41	倾盆大雨	傾盆大雨	qīngpéndàyǔ	heavy downpour, torrential rain
42	倾	傾	qīng	to overturn and pour out
43	料		liào	to expect, anticipate
44	撑伞	撐傘	chēngsǎn	to open, unfurl, hold an umbrella
45	不料		bùliào	unexpectedly
46	踩		cǎi	to step on
47	坑		kēng	pit, hole
48	稳	穩	wěn	steady, stable
49	摔		shuāi	to fall
50	爬		pá	to climb, scramble
51	爬起来	爬起來	páqǐlai	to get up

52	沾		zhān	to be stained with
53	花脸	花臉	huāliǎn	painted face (in Beijing opera)
54	溪		xī	stream, brook
55	像......般		xiàng . . . bān	same as, just like
56	直		zhí	continuously, straight,
57	立即		lìjí	immediately
58	积	積	jī	to accumulate, store up
59	滩	灘	tān	a puddle of, a pool of
60	不管怎样	不管怎樣	bùguǎn zěnyàng	whether or not, in any case
61	满脸的	滿臉的	mǎnliǎnde	all over the face
62	疑惑		yíhuò	doubt

2.3 Commentary 点评

这篇短文把一件平常的小事写得很丰满、很生动，靠的就是细节描写。

文中用了六个细节来写暴风雨，而且有递进关系。首先是对暴风雨的直接描写。其次是雨中的路况。第三个细节（伞吹喇叭）是暴风雨给"我"的下马威。第四、五个细节（摔跤和花脸）写出"我"在雨中的狼狈样子。第六个细节（脚下积水）是暴风雨的余波。这些细节对故事的发展起了很大的作用，

结尾出乎意外。虽然"我"白跑了一次，但他守信用和认真准备功课的品格却给读者留下了深刻的印象。

This short essay takes a simple occurrence and relies on careful attention to detail to portray it as very full and lively.

Within the piece, six details describe the rainstorm and gradually progress the plot. First is the rainstorm's direct description. Next is the condition of the road in the rain. The third detail (the umbrella turning inside out) is the storm showing "me" its power. The fourth and fifth details (falling over and the painted face) portray the appearance of "me" in a difficult position in the middle of the rainstorm. The sixth detail (a puddle at "my" feet) is the repercussion of the rainstorm. These six details greatly develop the story.

There is an unexpected ending. Although "I" went in vain, "my" qualities of keeping to "my" word and diligently preparing "my" homework truly give the reader a lasting impression.

词汇三

1	丰满	豐滿	fēngmǎn	full, plentiful
2	暴风雨	暴風雨	bàofēngyǔ	rainstorm, tempest
3	递进	遞進	dìjìn	to progressively move forward
4	路况	路況	lùkuàng	road condition
5	威		wēi	power, strength
6	下马威	下馬威	xiàmǎwēi	show of strength at first contact
7	狼狈	狼狽	lángbèi	in a difficult position; in a tight corner
8	余波		yúbō	repercussions, aftermath
9	出乎意外		chūhū yìwài	unexpected
10	白跑		báipǎo	to make a fruitless trip
11	品格		pǐngé	character, personality
12	深刻		shēnkè	deep, profound

2.4 Rhetoric 修辞

Metaphors and similes 比喻

比喻是常用的修辞手法。用比喻描写事物，可使事物形象鲜明生动，加深读者的印象；用来说明道理，能使道理通俗易懂。比喻是比较两个截然不同但又有相通之处的事物。

常见的比喻句如：

父爱如山，母爱如海。
西湖像一面明镜。
运动员像离弦的箭一样向终点跑去。
眼泪像断了线的珍珠。
心像玻璃一样碎了。

本课中的比喻句有："豆大的雨点从天空中落下来，像鞭子一样抽打着窗户。""你看，外边的路都成了黄河长江了，你何必出去呢？""一阵大风刮来，我的伞就吹了喇叭。""好不容易把伞翻过来，人早就成了落汤鸡。"

Metaphors and similes are commonly used rhetorical devices. Using metaphors and similes to describe things makes them more striking and lively and leaves a deeper impression. One may even use metaphors and similes to explain reason, and so may make reason more easily understandable by the masses. Metaphors and similes are used to compare two entirely different things which also have interlinking components.

Below are some examples of sentences with commonly seen metaphors and similes:

A father's love is like a mountain, and a mother's love is like the sea.
West Lake is like a mirror.
Athletes are like arrows shooting off to the finish line.
The tears were like an endless string of pearls.
The heart broke like glass.

This text also contains some sentences that use metaphors and similes: "Giant raindrops fell from the sky, and like a whip lashed the window." "Look, the roads outside have turned into the Yellow River and the Yangtze River, do you really need to go out?" "A large gust of wind came and blew my umbrella inside out like a trumpet." "With great difficulty I turned my umbrella back, and I instantly became soaked to the bone like a chicken drenched in water."

词汇四

1	比喻		bǐyù	metaphor or simile
2	鲜明	鮮明	xiānmíng	distinct, striking
3	通俗		tōngsú	popular, common, simple
4	截然不同		jiérán bùtóng	entirely different
5	相通		xiāngtōng	interlinked
6	弦		xián	bowstring, string
7	箭		jiàn	arrow

8	断	斷	duàn	to break
9	线	線	xiàn	thread, string
10	玻璃		bōli	glass
11	碎		suì	broken, broken into pieces

2.5　Practical writing 应用文

Congratulatory words 祝词

逢年过节或亲朋好友有高兴事儿时，我们常要写贺卡。参加喜庆活动，有时也要致贺词。中国人有很多吉祥的话，这里介绍几个传统的祝词贺语。

> 祝贺新年：新年快乐，万事如意
> 祝贺新婚：花好月圆，永结同心
> 祝贺生日：福如东海，寿比南山（一般用于年龄大的人）
> 祝贺新居：乔迁之喜
> 祝贺事业：大展宏图

此外，在毕业纪念册上，同学们也常常互相题写祝词贺语。这里也举几个例子。

> 毕业并不是结束，而是另一个旅途的开始。
> 每一个人都是自己幸福的建筑师。
> 快乐的秘诀不是做你所喜欢的事，而是喜欢你所做的事。
> 金银愈加磨练，色泽愈加光亮；人生愈加考验，生命愈加光辉。

When we celebrate the New Year or other festivals, or relatives and friends have good news, we often need to write greeting cards. Additionally, sometimes we need to give congratulatory addresses when participating in celebratory activities. Chinese people have many auspicious words, and here some traditional congratulatory words will be introduced:

> When congratulating people on the New Year, use "Happy New Year, may all your wishes come true!"
> When congratulating newlyweds, use "May your marriage be as blissful as beautiful flowers and the round moon, and may you be one soul everlasting!"
> When congratulating someone on his or her birthday, use "May your luck be as boundless as the Eastern Sea, and may you live as long as the Southern Mountain!" (generally used when greeting an elderly individual).
> When congratulating someone on moving to a new home, use "May you be happy in your new home!"
> When someone pursues a new career, use "Strive to make all of your biggest dreams come true!"

Furthermore, classmates often exchange words of congratulation in each other's yearbooks upon graduating. Here are a few examples:

> Graduation is not the end, but the beginning of another journey.
> Each person is the architect of his or her own happiness.
> The secret to happiness is not doing what you like but liking what you do.

Gold and silver are progressively tempered, and their luster becomes increasingly brighter; people are progressively tested, and their lives become increasingly fulfilling.

词汇五

1	祝词	祝詞	zhùcí	congratulatory expression/speech
2	逢		féng	to meet, encounter
3	逢年过节	逢年過節	féngnián guòjié	on New Year's Day or other festivals
4	贺卡	賀卡	hèkǎ	greeting card
5	致		zhì	to send, extend; make
6	贺词	賀詞	hècí	speech of congratulation
7	吉祥		jíxiáng	lucky, auspicious
8	万事如意	萬事如意	wànshìrúyì	everything goes as one wishes, "May all go well with you!"
9	结	結	jié	to tie, knot
10	福		fú	blessing, good fortune
11	寿	壽	shòu	longevity
12	乔迁	喬遷	qiáoqiān	to move to a better place
13	展		zhǎn	to put to good use, give free play to
14	宏		hóng	great, grand, magnificent
15	大展宏图	大展宏圖	dàzhǎn hóngtú	to realize one's ambition
16	纪念	紀念	jìniàn	to commemorate
17	册		cè	book, volume
18	纪念册	紀念冊	jìniàncè	commemorative album
19	题写	題寫	tíxiě	to write, inscribe
20	旅途		lǚtú	journey, trip
21	建筑师	建築師	jiànzhùshī	architect
22	秘诀	秘訣	mìjué	secret, trick
23	银	銀	yín	silver
24	愈加		yùjiā	increasingly, even more
25	磨练	磨練	móliàn	to cultivate, steel
26	色泽	色澤	sèzé	color and luster
27	考验	考驗	kǎoyàn	test, trial
28	光辉	光輝	guānghuī	brilliant, shining

2.6 Vocabulary training 词汇训练

一、填名词 Fill in the blanks with appropriate nouns to form adjective-noun phrases.

1 细微的 ____
2 细小的 ____
3 具体的 ____
4 细腻的 ____
5 平淡的 ____
6 丰富的 ____
7 狼狈的 ____
8 意外的 ____
9 深刻的 ____

10 常用的 ____
11 鲜明的 ____
12 通俗的 ____
13 易懂的 ____
14 不同的 ____
15 相通的 ____
16 吉祥的 ____

二、选词填空 Fill in the blanks correctly with the words provided.

1 一篇记事文，有了好的结构，还要注意 ____ 描写。

　　a. 细部　　c. 细心
　　b. 细节　　d. 细胞

2 只见概述不见描写，就显得语言枯燥，人物形象模糊，感情 ____ 。

　　a. 平常　　c. 平静
　　b. 平和　　d. 平淡

3 这些细节往往能对刻画人物形象和 ____ 文章主题起到很大的作用。

　　a. 深化　　c. 美化
　　b. 淡化　　d. 进化

4 中文课上，老师说明天要表演小品，并 ____ 我和马克一起准备。

　　a. 指挥　　c. 指定
　　b. 指导　　d. 指点

5 谁知，吃好晚饭 ____ 回到宿舍，突然窗外狂风大作，天上乌云翻滚。

　　a. 才　　　c. 一
　　b. 就　　　d. 刚

6 我跟马克打电话，想问他我们在哪儿见面，可是手机没 ____ 了。

　　a. 信息　　c. 信号
　　b. 信心　　d. 信用

7 你何必出去呢？马克也 ____ 呆在家里了。

　　a. 肯定　　c. 一定
　　b. 确定　　d. 决定

8 说罢，我鼓起勇气，拿把伞，____ 出门去。

　　a. 走　　　c. 跑
　　b. 冲　　　d. 跳

9 好不容易把伞翻过来，人早就成了落汤 ____ 。

　　a. 鸭　　　c. 鱼
　　b. 鸡　　　d. 虾

10 要是在这样的倾 ____ 大雨中，料他也跳不起来了。

    a. 碗   c. 缸
    b. 瓢   d. 盆

11 大风迎面 ____ 来，我只能把伞撑在胸前，低着头往前走。

    a. 吹   c. 刮
    b. 飘   d. 打

12 这时我的脸一定像 ____ 中的大花脸了。

    a. 歌剧   c. 戏剧
    b. 京剧   d. 音乐剧

13 这篇短文把一件 ____ 的小事写得很丰富、很生动。

    a. 正常   c. 经常
    b. 反常   d. 平常

14 他守信用和认真准备功课的品格给读者留下了 ____ 的印象。

    a. 深远   c. 深入
    b. 深刻   d. 深重

15 比喻是常用的修辞 ____ 。

    a. 办法   c. 手法
    b. 语法   d. 作法

16 西湖像一 ____ 明镜。

    a. 张   c. 个
    b. 面   d. 片

17 你尽可以根据你自己的情况和 ____ ，写出你自己的祝词贺语。

    a. 风格   c. 性格
    b. 品格   d. 人格

三、改错 Correct the errors.

1 中国古代哲学家孔子说过："天下大事，必作于细。"
2 突然窗外狂风翻滚，天上乌云大作。
3 随着一阵阵闪电和一道道雷声，豆大的雨点从天空中落下来。
4 说罢，我鼓起勇气，穿上雨衣，冲出门去。
5 大风迎面刮来，我只能把伞撑在头上。
6 走到马克的宿舍，身上的水像黄河长江般直往下流。
7 马克的同屋来开了门。一看是我，他满脸的喜悦。
8 第三个细节（伞吹喇叭）是暴风雨给"我"的见面礼。
9 用比喻说明道理，能使道理鲜明生动。
10 父爱如海，母爱如山。
11 福如南山，寿比东海。
12 运动员像离弦的箭一样向起点跑去。

2.7 Phrase training 语句训练

一、用句型造句 Make sentences using the following sentence patterns.

1 只见......不见

【课文例句】只见概述不见描写，更不见细节，就显得语言枯燥，人物形象模糊，感情平淡。
【生活例句】天气预报说今天要下暴雨，可是现在只见蓝天白云，不见一朵乌云，我们可以去海里游泳。

The weatherman said that today there would be a torrential downpour, but right now I only see a blue sky and white clouds, and there's not a dark cloud in the sky. We can go swim in the ocean.

2 不一定......也可以

【课文例句】这个"曲"字，在这儿不一定是"乐曲"的曲，也可以是"插曲"的曲。
【生活例句】这条鱼很新鲜，不一定用红烧的方法，也可以清蒸，那味道就更纯了。

This fish is very fresh. You don't necessarily have to cook it by braising it in soy sauce. You can also steam it, and the flavor will be even more savory.

3 随着

【课文例句】随着一道道闪电和一阵阵雷声，豆大的雨点从天空中落下来，像鞭子一样抽打着窗户。
【生活例句】随着经济的发展，越来越多的中国人出国旅行。你看，这里的游客几乎全是中国人。

As the economy developed, more and more Chinese people left the country to travel. Look, all of the tourists here are Chinese.

4 要是不......怎么

【课文例句】要是不排练，明天我们怎么表演呢？
【生活例句】要是不张嘴练习说中文，那你的中文怎么提高呢？

If you don't open your mouth to practice speaking Chinese, how will your Chinese improve?

5 好不容易

【课文例句】好不容易把伞翻过来，人早就成了落汤鸡。
【生活例句】黄佳佳要减肥，她好不容易减了三磅，但上星期去坐了一次豪华邮轮，又加了五磅。

Huang Jiajia wants to lose weight. She lost three pounds with great difficulty, but last week, she went on a cruise and gained five pounds again.

6 要是......不

【课文例句】要是在这样的倾盆大雨中，料他也跳不起来了。
【生活例句】要是你能每天复习一点的话，那今天就不用开夜车了。

If you review a little each day, then you won't need to study late into the night today.

7   靠的就是

【课文例句】这篇短文把一件平常的小事写得很丰富、很生动，靠的就是细节描写。

【生活例句】北京城里到处都是火锅店，可是"海底捞"的生意总是火红火红的，靠的就是服务态度好。

All over Beijing there are hotpot restaurants, but in "Haidi lao," business is always booming, and it's all because of the good-natured waiters.

8   虽然……但……却

【课文例句】虽然"我"白跑了一次，但他守信用和认真准备功课的品格却给读者留下了深刻的印象。

【生活例句】星期六我和朋友一起去爬了一天山。虽然很累，但很开心，山上的风景太美了。

On Saturday, my friend and I climbed a mountain all day. Although it was very tiring, it was very fun, and at the top of the mountain, we were able to see a beautiful view.

二、回答问题 Answer the questions.

1   一篇记事文，有了好的结构，还要注意什么？
2   什么是细节描写？
3   细节描写有什么作用？
4   明天的中文课上要做什么？
5   "我"和马克约好几点一起排练？
6   为什么他们没来得及说地点？
7   为什么"我"没法跟马克打电话？
8   为什么"我"一定要去马克的宿舍找他？
9   为什么"我"把伞撑在胸前？
10 "我"是怎么摔到水坑里去的？
11 为什么马克的同屋满脸的疑惑？
12 文中六个描写暴风雨的细节之间有一种什么关系？
13 用比喻描写事物和说明道理有什么好处？

三、选词填空，运用比喻手法完成句子 Fill in the blank with a word chosen from the parentheses to complete the sentences using metaphors and similes.

a   如果知识是海洋，我愿做条 ____ 在海洋里遨游；如果书本是天空，我愿做只 ____ 在空中翱翔。(船、鱼；小鸟、飞机)

b   爱心是一片冬日的阳光，使人感到温暖；爱心是 ____，使人感到 ____。（一阵春天的微风，一阵秋天的凉风；愉快、悲伤）

c   母亲是暑热中的阵阵清风，帮你拭去焦躁的汗水；母亲是困难时的一根拐杖，帮助你迈开前进的脚步；母亲是航行中的一个 ____ ，让你好好休息，再次扬起风帆。(车站、港湾)

d   老师，您是一座拱桥，我是从您弯曲的脊背上走过的学子；您是一张坚韧的弓，我是从弓里射出的一支 ____ 。(剑、箭)

e   书籍好比一架梯子，它能引导我们登上知识的殿堂。书籍如同一把钥匙，它能帮助我们打开知识的 ____ 。（窗户、大门）

2.8 Composition training 作文训练

一、仿写作文 *Imitative composition*

写一个题为《雨中曲》的故事，要符合以下三个要求：1. 故事要有趣；2. 注意细节描写；3. 用比喻。故事的长度不限。

Write a story titled "A Tune in the Rain" 雨中曲 following three requirements: 1. Write an interesting story. 2. Focus on details. 3. Use similes and metaphors. The length of the story is flexible.

二、情景作文 *Situational composition*

为《雨中曲》续写一个结尾。"我"听了马克的同屋的话后，回头去找马克。他们俩在半路上遇到了。

Write the ending to the story "A Tune in the Rain." After "I" heard what Mark's roommate said, "I" went back to find Mark. The two happened to meet in the middle.

三、串联作文 *Chain story composition*

这个练习是全班同学作为课外作业的集体创作。根据姓名的英文字母的排列，每人依次写一句。故事会放在"黑板"或其他类似的课堂教学管理系统的讨论板上。故事的开端提供在下面。尽量使故事易懂、逻性强辑和生动有趣。尽可能多用比喻。你一看到你前面的同学写好了，就应着手写作。一圈下来，轮到的任何人只要觉得故事应该到此为止，就可以结束故事。此后，班上要举行一次讨论。

This will be a collective story created by the whole class as homework. According to the alphabetical order of the class list, each writer is succeeded by the next student. The story will be posted on the discussion board on Blackboard© or a similar learning management system. The beginning of the story is provided below. Try to make the story understandable, logical, and interesting. Use metaphors to the best of your ability. You should begin to write your sentence as soon as you see the preceding one completed. After the first round, anybody during his or her turn can conclude the story if he or she thinks it is right place to do so. A class discussion of the story will follow.

题目：《烤肉野餐》

这个周末做什么？我们几个同学一商量：天气这么好，郊外烤肉去！说干就干，大家立即分工......

四、进阶作文 *Sequential composition*

以《进城》为题，写三篇短文。

Write three short pieces in sequence with the title of "Going to Town."

1 写一个100字左右的段落，简要地说明时间、事件和你进城的结果。

Write a paragraph of about 100 characters, briefly telling the time, events, and the result of your trip to town.

2   写两个100字左右的段落。每个段落要描写一个细节，比如你是怎么去的？你在城里做了些什么？发生了什么有趣的事？

Write a short piece with two paragraphs of about 100 characters each. Each one should narrate a detail. For example, how did you get there? What activities did you do in the town? Which people did you meet? What interesting things happened?

3   结合上述的三个段落的内容，写一个500字的小故事。要注意细节描写。

Combine the contents of the three aforementioned paragraphs and write a story of about 500 characters. Pay special attention to writing detailed descriptions.

五、应用文写作 *Practical writing*

我班的李丹梅是我们大学的辩论队的成员。今年我校荣获全国辩论大赛的冠军，我班要举行祝捷大会。大家选你致贺词。你将如何写你的祝词呢？

Li Danmei from our class is a member of our university's debate team. This year, our university came in first place at the national debate competition, and our class will have a celebration. Everyone has elected you to give a speech. How will you write your congratulatory words?

3 第三课 Writing about people
写人篇

3.1 Writing guide 写作指导

Capturing key traits 抓住特征

俗话说："画鬼容易画人难。"写人也不容易。要想把人写活，关键是要写出一个人的特点来。要不然，就会"千人一面"了。在外貌、动作、语言、性格各个方面，人和人之间总有不同的地方。

要找出一个人的特征，最有效的法子就是比较。比如，你要写爸爸，你可能觉得你的爸爸很普通，没什么特征。但如果你把爸爸和妈妈做一个比较，再跟你朋友的爸爸比一比，特点就很容易抓住了。

The saying goes: "It's easier to draw a ghost than a person." It's not easy to write about a person either. If you want to describe a person vividly, the key is to present his traits. Otherwise, it would be "One face for a thousand people." Different people always have distinct features in terms of appearance, movements, language, and characteristics.

In order to find out a person's traits, the most effective way is comparison to others. For example, if you want to write about your father, you may feel that your father is very ordinary, without any special features. However, if you compare your father with your mother, and also compare your father with your friend's father, it would be easy to grasp his special traits.

词汇一

1	抓住		zhuāzhù	to capture, grasp
2	特征		tèzhēng	feature, trait
3	俗话	俗話	súhuà	common saying
4	活		huó	lively, vivid
5	关键	關鍵	guānjiàn	key, crux
6	外貌		wàimào	appearance, looks
7	动作	動作	dòngzuò	movement, action
8	总	總	zǒng	without exception, always
9	有效		yǒuxiào	effective, valid
10	普通		pǔtōng	common, ordinary

3.2 Model text 范文

Mother's smiles 妈妈的微笑

【提示】妈妈和母爱可能是最常见的作文题目之一。你要抓住一个特点来写。可以自己定一个题目。这个特点也要反映在题目中。

Mothers and a mother's love are both possibly one of the most common topics for composition. You need to focus on portraying one trait. You can make your own title, but the trait that you choose to portray needs to be reflected in the title.

从我记事的时候起，妈妈的脸上总是挂着微笑。她笑的时候，两个嘴角微微上翘，两个大眼睛中也露着笑意。看到妈妈的微笑，我就觉得快乐、平静和安全。

上小学时，每天放学回家，迎接我的是妈妈的微笑。我从校车上下来，妈妈在车道旁等着。她抓起我的手，微笑地看着我，好像在问：今天过得好吗？

上中学时，我经常参加钢琴比赛或表演。当我从台侧走出来时，心跳得厉害，我就用眼角往观众席瞄一下。妈妈微笑着向我点点头，好像在说："别紧张，你会弹好的。"

上大学时，我每天给家里打视频电话。我把一天的情况告诉妈妈：今天考试考得怎样，又交了一个新朋友，等等。当我看到妈妈微笑地听着，我就觉得这一天过得不错。

妈妈也有不笑的时候。我小时候，有一次发高烧。妈妈坐在我的床边整整一个晚上没合过眼。她一会儿给我量体温，一会儿给我喝水，两眼红红的。到第二天早上，我的烧全退了，妈妈看了体温表，才露出了微笑。

还有一次，是我高中毕业的那一年。我的男朋友刚拿到驾照，非常高兴，要带我出去兜风。我们中午去麦当劳吃了午饭，又开车去沃尔玛购物，结果连下午的课都没上。老师打电话到家里问，妈妈才知道。那天回家时，妈妈脸上的笑容消失了。

妈妈的微笑是和煦的春风，是夏日的清泉，是长夜中的明星，是暴风雨中的港湾。我知道，在我前边漫长的生活道路上，妈妈的微笑会一直伴随着我。

- 微笑1：开篇
- 外貌描写：嘴角、眼睛
- 微笑2：小学，回家
- 动作描写：抓起手
- 微笑3：中学，比赛钢琴
- 语言描写："别紧张。"
- 微笑4：大学，视频电话
- 微笑5：发烧
- 微笑6：笑容没了
- 微笑7：排比
- 微笑8：结语

词汇二

1	微笑		wēixiào	smile
2	从 . . . 起	從 . . . 起	cóng . . . . . . qǐ	from . . . on
3	记事	記事	jìshì	to remember things
4	嘴角		zuǐjiǎo	corners of the mouth
5	微微		wēiwēi	slight, faint
6	翘	翹	qiào	to curl up, stick up
7	露		lù	to reveal, show
8	笑意		xiàoyì	faint smile
9	迎接		yíngjiē	to greet, welcome
10	车道	車道	chēdào	driveway
11	台侧	台側	táicè	side stage
12	眼角		yǎnjiǎo	corner of the eye
13	观众席	觀眾席	guānzhòngxí	auditorium (of a theater), grandstand (of a stadium)
14	席		xí	seat
15	瞄		miáo	to glance, glimpse
16	视频	視頻	shìpín	Internet video

17	发烧	發燒	fāshāo	to have a fever or temperature
18	量体温	量體溫	liángtǐwēn	to take one's temperature
19	体温表	體溫表	tǐwēnbiǎo	clinical thermometer
20	驾照	駕照	jiàzhào	driver's license
21	兜风	兜風	dōufēng	to go for a (joy) ride
22	麦当劳	麥當勞	màidāngláo	McDonald's
23	沃尔玛	沃爾瑪	wòěrmǎ	Walmart
24	笑容		xiàoróng	smiling expression, smile
25	消失		xiāoshī	to disappear, vanish
26	和煦		héxù	genial, pleasantly warm
27	泉		quán	spring, fountain
28	港湾	港灣	gǎngwān	harbor
29	漫长	漫長	màncháng	prolonged
30	伴随	伴隨	bànsuí	to accompany, follow

3.3 Commentary 点评

这位妈妈是个普通的妈妈，但作者抓住了她的特征（微笑），就写得很生动。妈妈的微笑象征着关爱（接车）、鼓励（弹琴）、倾听（电话）、帮助（发烧）和教育（缺课）。本文层层开掘，在平常中透出不平常。

最后的排比把文章推向高潮。四个排比句，每个又都是贴切的比喻。"和煦的春风"使人身心愉快，"夏日的清泉"送来急需的物品，"长夜中的明星"在困惑中指出方向，"暴风雨中的港湾"提供安全和保护。这不是对妈妈的微笑的最好的解读吗？

This is an ordinary mother, but the author focuses on her special trait – her smile, which the author wrote about very vividly. Her mother's smile symbolizes love (conveyed when she picks her up at the bus stop), encouragement (seen when she is playing the piano at the recital), attentiveness (conveyed during the video chat), assistance and support (when the author has a fever), and instruction and guidance (when the author skips class). This article delves deeper layer by layer and uncovers unusual elements of ordinary things.

The parallelisms at the end of the article propelled the story to its climax. Each of the four paralleled sentences is also an appropriate metaphor. A "mild spring breeze" makes people physically and mentally content, a "clear spring in the summer" delivers necessary things, a "bright star in the long night" points in the right direction in a time of confusion, and a "harbor in the storm" provides safety and protection. Aren't these the best descriptions of a mother's smile?

词汇三

1	关爱	關愛	guān'ài	love and care
2	倾听	傾聽	qīngtīng	to listen attentively to
3	缺课	缺課	quēkè	to be absent from class
4	开掘	開掘	kāijué	to dig, (of literature) deeply explore and fully express
5	透出		tòuchū	to reveal, show
6	排比		páibǐ	parallelism, parallel sentences
7	高潮		gāocháo	climax
8	贴切	貼切	tiēqiè	(of words) appropriate, proper
9	急需		jíxū	to be badly in need of
10	物品		wùpǐn	goods
11	困惑		kùnhuò	puzzled, confused
12	提供		tígōng	to provide, supply
13	解读	解讀	jiědú	interpretation, explanation

3.4 Rhetoric 修辞

Parallelism 排比

排比，就是把三个或者三个以上结构相似、意义相关、语气相近的词组或者句子排列在一起。排比句读起来琅琅上口，气势很盛，能增强文章的表达效果。

用排比写人，能将人物刻画细致。用排比写景，能将景物描绘生动。用排比说理，道理能说得充分透彻。用排比抒情，感情会显得强烈奔放。

比如，"桃树、杏树、梨树，都开满了花，红的像火，粉的像霞，白的像雪。" 这个句子用了三个相同的句式描写花的各种色彩，就是排比。

本课中最后一段的 "妈妈的微笑是和煦的春风，是夏日的清泉，是长夜中的明星，是暴风雨中的港湾" 也是一个精彩的排比。

Paibi (parallelism) refers to placing together three or more phrases or sentences with analogous structure, related meaning, and similar mood. When reading the *paibi* sentences, they are easily read and sound catchy, producing strong momentum and thus strengthening the article's expressiveness.

Using *paibi* to write about people, one can depict characters exquisitely; using *paibi* to write about scenery, one can describe scenes vividly; using *paibi* to reason, one can present ideas logically, using *paibi* to express feelings, one can release a powerful and unrestrained flood of emotions.

For example, "Peach trees, apricot trees, and pear trees are all in full bloom. The red is like fire, the pink is like rosy clouds, and the white is like snow." This sentence uses three phrases with similar structure to describe different colors of flowers, and this is a *paibi*.

In the last paragraph of the main text, a "mother's smile is a mild spring breeze, is a clear spring in the summer, is a bright star in the long night, and is a harbor in the storm" is also a wonderful *paibi*.

词汇四

1	相关	相關	xiāngguān	related, interrelated
2	琅琅上口		lángláng shàngkǒu	easy to read out
3	气势	氣勢	qìshì	momentum, impetus
4	盛		shèng	vigorous, energetic
5	增强	增強	zēngqiáng	to strengthen, enhance
6	效果		xiàoguǒ	effect, result
7	细致	細致	xìzhì	careful, exquisite
8	充分		chōngfèn	full, sufficient
9	透彻	透徹	tòuchè	penetrating, thorough
10	强烈	強烈	qiángliè	strong, powerful, intense
11	奔放		bēnfàng	(of thoughts, feelings, style of writing, etc.) bold and unrestrained
12	桃		táo	peach
13	杏		xìng	apricot
14	梨		lí	pear
15	粉		fěn	pink
16	霞		xiá	rosy clouds, morning or evening glow

3.5 Practical writing 应用文

感谢信 *Letter of gratitude*

如果你得到一个人或一个机构的比较重要的帮助，比如一位老师给你写了推荐信或者一个基金会授予你奖学金，你就需要写一封感谢信。

　　感谢信的篇幅不用太长，但要注意几点。一是要说明写信的原由。这个人或机构对你提供了什么帮助，并给你的生活或事业带来什么好处都要简要地写清楚。二是感谢的话要写得诚恳、有感情，不能简单地说一声谢谢就了结。

If you receive relatively important help from a person or an organization, for example, a professor who wrote a letter of recommendation for you or a foundation that awarded you a scholarship, you need to write a letter of gratitude.

A letter of gratitude should not be lengthy, but you need to pay attention to a few points. First, you need to tell the reasons for writing the letter. You need to write succinctly about what kind of help that person or organization has provided to you, and what benefit to your life or career resulted from that help. Secondly, the words of gratitude should be sincere and expressive – simply saying a quick thank you will not be enough.

词汇五

1	推荐	推薦	tuījiàn	to recommend, nominate
2	基金会	基金會	jījīnhuì	foundation
3	基金		jījīn	fund
4	授予		shòuyǔ	to grant, confer
5	奖学金	獎學金	jiǎngxuéjīn	scholarship, fellowship
6	篇幅		piānfú	length of an article
7	原由		yuányóu	cause, reason
8	事业	事業	shìyè	career, profession
9	诚恳	誠懇	chéngkěn	sincere, earnest
10	了结	了結	liǎojié	to finish, settle up

3.6 Vocabulary training 词汇训练

一、填形容词 Fill in the blanks with appropriate adjectives to form adjective-noun phrases.

1　____ 的外貌
2　____ 的动作
3　____ 的语言
4　____ 的性格
5　____ 的特征
6　____ 的地方
7　____ 的微笑
8　____ 的题目
9　____ 的眼睛
10　____ 的笑意
11　____ 的比赛

12 ＿＿＿ 的表演
13 ＿＿＿ 的春风
14 ＿＿＿ 的港湾
15 ＿＿＿ 的生活
16 ＿＿＿ 的道路
17 ＿＿＿ 的鼓励
18 ＿＿＿ 的帮助
19 ＿＿＿ 的教育
20 ＿＿＿ 的排比
21 ＿＿＿ 的比喻
22 ＿＿＿ 的语气
23 ＿＿＿ 的效果
24 ＿＿＿ 的景物
25 ＿＿＿ 的感情
26 ＿＿＿ 的机构

二、选词填空 Fill in the blanks with the words provided.

1 要找出一个人的特征，最 ＿＿＿ 的法子就是比较。

   a. 有效   c. 有力
   b. 有益   d. 有利

2 看到妈妈的微笑，我就觉得快乐、＿＿＿ 和安全。

   a. 安静   c. 平静
   b. 冷静   d. 清静

3 她 ＿＿＿ 起我的手，微笑地看着我，好像在问：今天过得好吗？

   a. 握   c. 提
   b. 抬   d. 抓

4 当我从台 ＿＿＿ 走出来时，心跳得厉害。

   a. 边   c. 前
   b. 旁   d. 侧

5 到第二天早上，我的烧全 ＿＿＿ 了。

   a. 退   c. 走
   b. 逃   d. 跑

6 我的男朋友刚拿到驾照，非常高兴，要带我出去 ＿＿＿。

   a. 兜风   c. 望风
   b. 放风   d. 避风

7 那天回家时，妈妈脸上的笑容 ＿＿＿ 了。

   a. 消灭   c. 消失
   b. 消化   d. 消费

8 妈妈的微笑是和煦的 ＿＿＿ 风，是夏日的清泉。

    a. 春   c. 秋
    b. 夏   d. 冬

9 妈妈的微笑象征着 ＿＿＿ 、鼓励、倾听、帮助和教育。

    a. 友爱   c. 可爱
    b. 热爱   d. 关爱

10 最后的排比把文章 ＿＿＿ 向高潮。

    a. 拉   c. 抬
    b. 推   d. 拍

11 这不是对妈妈的微笑的最好的 ＿＿＿ 吗？

    a. 阅读   c. 解读
    b. 朗读   d. 攻读

12 感谢的话要写得 ＿＿＿ 、有感情。

    a. 诚实   c. 诚心
    b. 诚恳   d. 诚信

三、改错 Correct the errors.

1 俗话说: "画人容易画鬼难。"
2 要想把人写活，关键是要写出一个人的特色来。
3 在外貌、动作、语言、性格各个方面，人和人之间就有不同的地方。
4 比如，你要写爸爸，你可能觉得你的爸爸很普遍，没什么特征。
5 她笑的时候，两个眼角微微上翘，两个大眼睛中也挂着笑意。
6 上小学时，每天放学回家，接待我的是妈妈的微笑。
7 当我从台侧走出来时，心跳得利害，我就用眼角往观众席瞄一下。
8 我小时候，有一次发高温。
9 妈妈看了温度表，才露出了微笑。
10 我的男朋友刚拿到护照，非常高兴，要带我出去兜风。
11 在我前边漫长的生活道路上，妈妈的微笑会一直跟随着我。
12 "暴风雨中的港湾" 提倡安全和保护。
13 排比句读起来琅琅上口，气势很盛，能增强文章的表示效果。

3.7 Phrase training 语句训练

一、用句型造句 Make sentences using the following sentence patterns.

1 ......要不然

【课文例句】要想把人写活，关键是要写出一个人的特点来。要不然，就会 "千人一面" 了。
【生活例句】很多中国人不吃奶酪，所以今天中国代表团来，不要带他们去意大利饭店吃饭，要不然，有些中国客人要挨饿了。

Many Chinese people don't eat cheese. Therefore, for today's Chinese delegation, do not take them to an Italian restaurant. Otherwise, some of our Chinese guests would be hungry.

2 如果……就

【课文例句】但如果你把爸爸和妈妈做一个比较，再跟你朋友的爸爸比一比，特点就很容易抓住了。

【生活例句】王平的的爸爸答应他，如果他能进一所好大学，就给他买一辆本田汽车。

Wang Ping's dad promised him that if he can get into a good college, he will award him with a Honda.

3 从……起

【课文例句】从我记事的时候起，妈妈的脸上总是挂着微笑。

【生活例句】张丽华从八岁起就开始打网球，现在已经打了十二年了。她打得非常棒，是我们大学女队的队长。

Zhang Lihua started to play tennis when she was 8 years old and has already played for 12 years. She plays extremely well, and she is the captain of the women's tennis team of our university.

4 当……时

【课文例句】当我从台侧走出来时，心跳得厉害，我就用眼角往观众席瞄一下。

【生活例句】当我收拾好我的包准备离开办公室时，我的经理又走过来给了我一份材料要我立即处理一下。唉，真累啊.

When I picked up my bag and prepared to leave the office, my manager came to me again. He gave me a document and asked me to work on it. Well, this is really tiring.

5 一会儿……一会儿

【课文例句】她一会儿给我量体温，一会儿给我喝水，两眼红红的。

【生活例句】你做功课时一会儿看手机，一会儿看电视，怎么做得好呢？

When you do your homework, sometimes you look at your cellphone, and sometimes you watch TV. How can you do well?

6 ……才

【课文例句】妈妈看了体温表，才露出了微笑。

【生活例句】我出国多年没回去，老听人说上海现在有多大多漂亮，但不能想象。今年夏天去了一次，才为上海的变化而震撼。

I left China many years ago, and I haven't been back since then. I had always heard about how big and how beautiful Shanghai is now, but I couldn't imagine it. It was only when I went back this summer that I was shocked by the changes that had taken place in Shanghai.

7 ……结果

【课文例句】我们中午去麦当劳吃了午饭，又开车去沃尔玛购物，结果连下午的课都没上。

【生活例句】王玉今天睡过了头，匆匆忙忙赶去上八点的中文课，结果到了教室一坐下，打开书包，发现没带中文课本！

Wang Yu overslept today and she had to rush to the 8 o'clock Chinese class. As a result, only when she came to the classroom, sat down and opened her backpack, did she find that she hadn't brought her Chinese textbook!

8   ……但……就

【课文例句】这位妈妈是个普通的妈妈，但作者抓住了她的特征（微笑），就写得很生动。

【生活例句】周庄以前是上海附近的一个普通的小镇，但经过开发，就变成一个富有江南水乡特点的旅游景点。

Zhouzhuang used to be an ordinary small village near Shanghai. However, after development, it became a tourist hot spot with the region's rich features of rivers and lakes south of the Yangtze River.

9   这不是……吗

【课文例句】这不是对妈妈的微笑的最好的解读吗？

【生活例句】这个城市虽然不大，但有青山绿水，气候也很好，这不是跟咱们老家很像的吗？

Although this city is not big, it has green hills and clear waters, and the weather is very nice too. Doesn't it look like our hometown very much?

二、回答问题 Answer the questions.

1   在哪些方面，人和人之间总有不同的地方？
2   要找出一个人的特征，最有效的法子是什么？
3   妈妈笑的时候是什么样子？
4   看到妈妈的微笑，"我"就觉得怎么样？
5   上小学时，"我"每天放学回家，妈妈在哪儿等她？
6   上大学时，"我"每天是怎么给家里打电话的？
7   "我"每天给家里打电话时，告诉妈妈什么？
8   "我"发高烧时，妈妈坐在她床边做什么？
9   "我"的男朋友为什么要带她出去兜风？
10 他们为什么连下午的课都没上？
11 为什么作者能把一位普通的妈妈写得很生动？
12 排比是一种怎样的修辞手段？
13 用排比写人、写景和说理有些什么好处？
14 本课课文中，哪里用了排比？

三、运用排比手法完成句子 Complete the sentences using personification.

1   填空 Fill in the blanks.

a. 欣赏高山，就会像高山一样沉着坚强；____ 大树，就会像大树一样自尊自立；欣赏小草，就会像 ____ 一样充满希望。

b. 要记住：不是每一颗种子都能长成大树，不是每一颗水珠都能流进 ____ ，不是每一个生命都能焕发光彩。

c. 不要放弃希望。希望使人保持乐观的情绪，希望帮助人克服眼前的 ____ ，希望引领人走向光明的 ____ 。

2　模仿：仿照例句，完成排比句　Make sentences with parallelism, following sample sentences.

    d.　钱能买到书籍，却买不到知识；钱能买到时装，却买不到美丽；钱能买到玫瑰，却买不到爱情；钱能买到药品，却买不到健康 ；钱能买到 ____ ，却买不到 ____ 。

    e.　人生的意义在于奉献。如果你是一棵大树，就撒下一片阴凉；如果你是一泓清泉，就滋润一方土地；如果你是 ____ ，就 ____ 。

    f.　幸福是什么？其实很简单。一壶清茶,可以品出幸福的滋味；一朵鲜花，可以带来幸福的气息；一本好书，可以 ____ 。

    g.　种子，如果害怕埋没，那它永远不会发芽；鲜花，如果害怕凋谢，那它永远不会开花；航船，如果 ____ ，那它永远 ____ 。

3.8 Composition training 作文训练

一、仿写作文 *Imitative composition*

写一篇题目跟《妈妈的微笑》类似的文章，要符合以下三个要求：1. 写一个你熟悉的人；2. 写一个他（她）的主要特征很明显的典型的场景；3. 用上排比的手法。文章的长度不限。

Write an article with a title similar to "Mother's Smiles" following three requirements: 1. Write about a person you are familiar with. 2. Describe the typical situations when his/her key traits are obvious. 3. Use *paibi* (parallelism). The length of the article is flexible.

二、情景作文 *Situational composition*

《妈妈的微笑》倒数第二段的最后一个句子是： "那天回家时，妈妈脸上的笑容消失了。" 请接下去写一个关于妈妈和 "我" 对话的段落，并保持微笑的主题。

The last sentence of the second to last paragraph in "Mother's Smiles" reads: "When I came back home that day, the smile disappeared from mother's face." Please write a paragraph continued from this sentence, presenting the dialogue between mother and "I," which should contain the motif of the smile.

三、串联作文 *Chain story composition*

这个练习是全班同学作为课外作业的集体创作。根据姓名的英文字母的排列，每人依次写一句。文章会放在 "黑板" 或其他类似的课堂教学管理系统的讨论板上。文章的开端提供在下面。尽量使文章易懂、逻性强辑和生动有趣。尽可能多用排比句。你一看到你前面的同学写好了，就应着手写作。一圈下来，轮到的任何人只要觉得故事应该到此为止，就可以结束故事。此后，班上要举行一次讨论。

This will be a collective story created by the whole class as homework. According to the alphabetical order of the class list, every writer is succeeded by the next student. The article will be posted on the discussion board on Blackboard© or a similar learning management system. The beginning of the article is provided below. Try to make the story understandable, logical, and interesting. Use parallelism to the best of your ability. You should begin to write your sentence as soon as you see the preceding one completed. After the first round, anybody can conclude the story if he or she thinks it is right place to do so. A class discussion of the story will follow.

题目：《我的一年级中文老师》

记得我第一次走进一年级中文教室的时候，心里非常好奇，也有些紧张：我的中文老师会是什么样的一个人呢？他会不会特别严厉呢？正想着呢，只见一位年轻的女老师走进教室......

四、进阶作文 *Sequential composition*

以《我的同学》为题，写三篇短文。

Write three short pieces in sequence with the title of "My Classmate."

1　写一个100字左右的段落，描写你的一个同学的主要特征，可以是他的表情（比如微笑）、习惯（比如整洁）或别的。

　　Write a paragraph of about 100 characters, describing your classmate's main trait, which can be his expression (such as a smile), habit (such as neatness) or something else.

2　写两个100字左右的段落，分别叙述这个特征的例子。

　　Write a short piece with two 100-character paragraphs, each telling one example of this trait.

3　结合上述的三个段落的内容，写一篇500字的短文，介绍你的同学的特征。

　　Combine the contents of the three aforementioned paragraphs, and write a report of about 500 characters, presenting your classmate's main trait.

五、应用文写作 *Practical composition*

一位教授给你写了一封推荐信。你因此而得到了你申请的暑期工作。请给这位教授写一封感谢信。

A professor wrote a letter of recommendation for you. As a result, you secured the summer job you applied for. Please write a letter of gratitude to this professor.

4 第四课　Writing about scenery, part one
绘景篇上

4.1 Writing guide 写作指导

Careful observations 仔细观察

要写好景，重要的是要仔细观察所写的景物。在观察时，要善于抓住不同季节、不同时间、不同气候、不同地区中景物呈现出的颜色、形态、声响、气味等方面的特征和变化。

　　比如，一年有春、夏、秋、冬四季，不同季节的景观大不相同。在一天中，清晨、白天、黄昏、夜晚等不同时段给景物涂上了不同的色彩。同一景物在风、雨、雾、雪中所展现的姿态也各不相同。南方、北方、城市、乡村、高原、平地等不同的地区，也有着各自不同的景物特征。把观察到的景物特征用生动的文字记录下来，就是一篇出色的写景文章。

In order to write eloquently about scenery, it's important to carefully observe the scenery you want to describe. During observation, you should skillfully capture the features and transformations of the colors, shapes, sounds, smells, and other aspects that the scenery displays in different seasons, different times, different weather, and different places.

For example, there are the four seasons of spring, summer, autumn, and winter in a year; the scenery varies greatly in different seasons. In one day, different time periods such as dawn, day, twilight, and evening paint scenes with different colors. The same scenery appears differently in wind, rain, fog or snow. Different regions including south and north, cities and rural areas, and plateaus and plains have their own distinct features. Recording what you have observed with vivid language would be a wonderful article of scenery writing.

词汇一

1	绘景	繪景	huìjǐng	scenery description
2	绘	繪	huì	to paint, describe
3	仔细	仔細	zǐxì	careful, attentive
4	观察	觀察	guānchá	to observe, watch
5	景物		jǐngwù	scenery
6	善于		shànyú	to be good at
7	呈现	呈現	chéngxiàn	to present, appear
8	形态	形態	xíngtài	shape, form
9	声响	聲響	shēngxiǎng	sound
10	气味	氣味	qìwèi	smell, scent
11	景观	景觀	jǐngguān	sights, landscape
12	涂	塗	tú	to apply, smear

13	雾	霧	wù	fog
14	姿态	姿態	zītài	gesture, posture
15	高原		gāoyuán	plateau
16	地区		dìqū	area, region
17	出色		chūsè	outstanding, remarkable

4.2 Model text 范文

Impressions of Niagara Falls 尼亚加拉观瀑记

【提示】选一个你游览过的地方写一篇游记，自己起一个题目。要从不同的角度写景。尽可能多用一些修辞手法，特别是夸张。描写的时候也要适当用一些形容词。

Write a travel journal about a place you have been to and make your own title. Write about scenery from different angles. Try to use many literary devices, especially exaggeration. Use adjectives appropriately for description.

今年暑假，我们全家去观看尼亚加拉大瀑布。开车经过美加边境的水牛城，不久就能望见世界闻名的大瀑布了。远远望去，它像一幅白练，挂在青山绿水之间。难怪其中的一块瀑布叫 "新娘面纱" 呢。
- 远望
- 比喻

到了大瀑布附近，我们先乘 "雾中少女" 号游船观赏瀑布。瀑布就在我们面前倾泻下来，我不禁想起中文课上学过的李白写瀑布的名句："飞流直下三千尺，疑是银河落九天。" 这时，看到的只是奔流的瀑布、飞溅的浪花和弥漫的水汽。听到的只是轰鸣的水声和船上游客的惊叫和欢呼声。船开到瀑布前的时候，只觉得天地之间只有瀑布存在，我也已化为其中的一颗水珠了。
- 乘船观赏
- 夸张

下船后，我们又去参观加拿大境内的 "瀑布后之旅"。搭乘电梯降到几十米深的地下，沿着隧道来到突出的平台上，突然发现瀑布就在身旁！嗨，《西游记》中孙悟空的水帘洞不就是这样的吗？暴风雨劈头盖脸地打来，成语 "瓢泼大雨"、"倾盆大雨" 都显得太轻飘了。这哪里是一瓢水、一盆水呀？这简直是一个巨人把五大湖翻转过来，把水都倒下来了。
- 夸张
- 瀑布后观赏
- 联想

尼亚加拉瀑布在入夜后则是另一番景象。在周围五颜六色的聚光灯的照耀下，它显得比白天更多姿多彩。瀑布就像亿万颗珍珠，随着灯光变换颜色。由雪白转为粉红，由粉红转为天蓝，由天蓝转为草绿，五彩缤纷，千变万化，雄伟的瀑布变成一种神奇的仙境。
- 夸张
- 夜景
- 比喻

词汇二

1	尼亚加拉	尼亞加拉	níyàjiālā	Niagara
2	瀑		pù	waterfall
3	游记	遊記	yóujì	travel notes, travel journal
4	角度		jiǎodù	angle, point of view
5	尽可能	盡可能	jǐnkěnéng	as far as possible, to the best of one's ability
6	手法		shǒufǎ	technique, skill
7	夸张	誇張	kuāzhāng	exaggeration

8	适当	適當	shìdàng	properly, appropriately
9	形容词	形容詞	xíngróngcí	adjective
10	瀑布		pùbù	waterfall
11	加		jiā	加拿大（简称）, Canada
12	边境	邊境	biānjìng	border, frontier
13	水牛		shuǐniú	buffalo
14	水牛城		shuǐniúchéng	Buffalo (city)
15	世界闻名	世界聞名	shìjiè wénmíng	world-renowned
16	幅		fú	*a measure word for cloth, painting, etc.*
17	练	練	liàn	white silk
18	其中		qízhōng	among
19	新娘面纱	新娘面紗	xīnniáng miànshā	"Bridal Veil Falls"
20	雾中少女	霧中少女	wùzhōng shāonǚ	"Maid of the Mist"
21	观赏	觀賞	guānshǎng	观看欣赏
22	倾泻	傾瀉	qīngxiè	to rush down in torrent, pour down
23	李白		lǐbái	poet (701–762)
24	疑		yí	to suspect
25	银河	銀河	yínhé	the Milky Way
26	九天		jiǔtiān	the Ninth Heaven, highest of heavens
27	奔流		bēnliú	to flush, rush
28	飞溅	飛濺	fēijiàn	to splash, spatter
29	浪花		lànghuā	spray, spindrift
30	弥漫	彌漫	mímàn	to permeate, diffuse
31	水汽		shuǐqì	vapor, steam, moisture
32	轰鸣	轟鳴	hōngmíng	to roar, thunder
33	惊叫	驚叫	jīngjiào	to scream, yell
32	欢呼	歡呼	huānhū	to cheer, hail
33	存在		cúnzài	to exist
34	化		huà	to turn, transform
35	颗	顆	kē	*a measure word for grains and grain-like objects*
36	水珠		shuǐzhū	drop of water
37	境		jìng	territory
38	瀑布后之旅	瀑布後之旅	pùbùhòu zhīlǚ	"Journey behind the Falls"
39	搭乘		dāchéng	to ride
40	电梯	電梯	diàntī	elevator
41	降		jiàng	to go down, fall; drop
42	隧道		suìdào	tunnel
43	突出		tūchū	protruding, projecting
44	平台		píngtái	terrace, platform
45	西游记	西遊記	xīyóujì	*Journey to the West*
46	孙悟空	孫悟空	Sūn Wùkōng	a character in *The Journey to the West*, Monkey King
47	水帘洞	水簾洞	shuǐliándòng	the Water Curtain Cave, where Sun Wukong resides
48	劈头盖脸	劈頭蓋臉	pītóu gàiliǎn	right in the face
49	瓢		piáo	gourd ladle
50	泼	潑	pō	to splash, spill
51	瓢泼大雨	瓢潑大雨	piáopō dàyǔ	pouring rain
52	轻飘	輕飄	qīngpiāo	light, fluffy
53	巨人		jùrén	giant

54	五大湖		wǔdàhú	the Great Lakes
55	翻转	翻轉	fānzhuǎn	to overturn
56	则	則	zé	yet, though
57	另一番		lìngyīfān	different, another kind of
58	景象		jǐngxiàng	scene, sight
59	五颜六色	五顏六色	wǔyánliùsè	colorful
60	聚光灯	聚光燈	jùguāngdēng	spotlight
61	照耀		zhàoyào	to illuminate, shine
62	多姿多彩		duōzī duōcǎi	charming and colorful
63	变换	變換	biànhuàn	to transform, switch
64	粉红	粉紅	fěnhóng	pink
65	天蓝	天藍	tiānlán	sky-blue, azure
66	草绿	草綠	cǎolǜ	grass-green
67	五彩缤纷	五彩繽紛	wǔcǎi bīnfēn	colorful
68	千变万化	千變萬化	qiānbiàn wànhuà	ever-changing
69	雄伟	雄偉	xióngwéi	majestic
70	神奇		shénqí	magical, wonderful
71	仙		xiān	immortal, fairy
72	仙境		xiānjìng	fairyland

4.3 Commentary 点评

本文从四个角度观察、描写大瀑布：先是远望，再从 "雾中少女" 船上看，然后到瀑布后看，最后是写夜景。这篇游记写得很具体，也很实在，可以把它当作导游手册呢。

　　本文用了很多不同的修辞手法，特别是比喻和夸张。此外，也用了很多形容词。有写色彩的，如 "雪白"、"粉红"、"天蓝"、"草绿"；有比较文雅的，如 "雄伟"、"神奇"；有把动词作形容词的，如 "奔流"、"飞溅"、"弥漫"、"轰鸣"；也有用四字成语作形容词的，如 "五颜六色"、"多姿多彩"、"五彩缤纷"、"千变万化" 等等。

The author observed and described the great falls from four perspectives. First, he watched from distance. Then he looked at it from the "Maid of the Mist" boat. Next, he observed from behind the falls. Finally, he described the scene at night. This travel journal is very detailed and also realistic, so we may even use it as a tour guide.

This article used many different rhetorical devices, particularly metaphor and exaggeration. Additionally, it also used many adjectives. Some are about colors, such as 雪白 (snow white), 粉红 (pink), 天蓝 (sky-blue) and 草绿 (grass-green). Some are relatively sophisticated, such as 雄伟 (majestic) and 神奇 (magical). Some are verbs used as adjectives, such as 奔流 (rushing), 飞溅 (splashing), 弥漫 (permeating), and 轰鸣 (roaring). Some are four-character idioms used as adjectives such as 五颜六色 (colorful), 多姿多彩 (charming and colorful), 五彩缤纷 (multicolored), and 千变万化 (ever-changing).

词汇三

| 1 | 手册 | 手冊 | shǒucè | manual, handbook |
| 2 | 文雅 | | wényǎ | elegant, refined |

4.4 Rhetoric 修辞

Exaggeration 夸张

夸张是运用丰富的想象力，在现实的基础上有目的地放大或缩小事物的形象特征，以增强表达效果的修辞手法。比如：

> 他的嗓子像铜钟一样，十里地外都能听见。
> 教室里静得连根针掉在地上也听得到。
> 这块巴掌大的地方,怎么能盖房子呢？
> 嗓子干得直冒烟，我能喝它一条江。

　　本课中引用的李白的诗句 "飞流直下三千尺" 是一个典型的夸张的例子。此外，"只觉得天地之间只有瀑布存在，我也已化为其中的一颗水珠了" 巧妙地把两个夸张（瀑布的放大和 "我" 的缩小）放在一起来形容瀑布的气势。

Exaggeration is a rhetorical device which, on the basis of reality, uses rich imagination to purposefully enlarge or reduce the features of something in order to enhance the expressiveness of the author. For example:

> His voice is like a copper bell which can be heard beyond ten miles.
> It's so quiet in the classroom that you may even hear the sound of a needle dropping on the floor.
> How can one build a house on this palm-sized land?
> My throat is so dry that it's burning and I can drink a whole river.

　　Li Bai's line cited in this lesson: "The flying flow of water rushing straight down for three thousand miles" is a typical example of exaggeration. In addition, the line of "I felt that only the falls existed between heaven and earth and I had already transformed into a water drop of the falls" skillfully combines two exaggerations (the enlarged falls and reduced "I") to describe the momentum of the falls.

词汇四

1	运用	運用	yùnyòng	to utilize, apply
2	现实	現實	xiànshí	reality
3	基础	基礎	jīchǔ	base, basis
4	目的		mùdì	purpose, intention; goal
5	放大		fàngdà	to enlarge, magnify
6	缩小	縮小	suōxiǎo	to reduce, shrink
7	嗓子		sǎngzi	throat, voice
8	铜	銅	tóng	copper, bronze
9	钟	鐘	zhōng	bell
10	掉		diào	to drop, fall
11	巴掌		bāzhǎng	palm, hand
12	盖	蓋	gài	to build, construct
13	冒烟	冒煙	màoyān	to fume, smoke
14	引用		yǐnyòng	to cite, quote
15	典型		diǎnxíng	typical, representative
16	巧妙		qiǎomiào	ingenious, smart, clever

4.5 Practical writing 应用文

Posters 海报

海报一般是用来向群众介绍各种活动（文艺演出、体育比赛、学术报告、社团活动等）的消息。海报可在公共场所张贴，也可做成电子邮件的附件，通过网络传播。

海报中通常要用简明扼要的语言写清楚活动的主题和内容，主办单位，以及时间和地点。设计要新颖美观，才能吸引眼球。在电子时代，每个人都能自己动手，设计精美的海报。

Posters are usually used to inform the masses of various events, such as art performances, sports competitions, scholarly talks, community events, etc. Posters can be posted in public places and can also be attached to emails and disseminated throughout the Internet.

Posters often use succinct language to clearly present the theme and content of the event, the host organization, as well as the time and place. The design should be unique and artistic in order to attract the eye of a passerby. In this electronic age, everyone can create one by his or herself and design exquisite and beautiful posters.

词汇五

1	海报	海報	hǎibào	poster
2	群众	群衆	qúnzhòng	mass, common people, general public
3	文艺	文藝	wényì	literature and art
4	演出		yǎnchū	show, performance
5	学术	學術	xuéshù	learning, academics
6	社团	社團	shètuán	mass organizations, association
7	消息		xiāoxi	news, message
8	场所	場所	chǎngsuǒ	location, site
9	张贴	張貼	zhāngtiē	to post, put up
10	附件		fùjiàn	attachment
11	网络	網絡	wǎngluò	network
12	传播	傳播	chuánbō	to spread, disseminate
13	通常		tōngcháng	generally, commonly, usually
14	主办	主辦	zhǔbàn	to sponsor, host
15	以及		yǐjí	along with, as well as
16	设计	設計	shèjì	design
17	新颖	新穎	xīnyǐng	new, novel
18	美观	美觀	měiguān	beautiful, artistic
19	吸引		xīyǐn	to attract
20	眼球		yǎnqiú	eyeball
21	动手	動手	dòngshǒu	to get to work, to do
22	精美		jīngměi	exquisite

4.6 Vocabulary training 词汇训练

一、填形容词 Fill in the blanks with appropriate adjectives to form adjective-noun phrases.

1 ____ 的观察
2 ____ 的景物
3 ____ 的季节
4 ____ 的气候

5 ____ 的地区
6 ____ 的颜色
7 ____ 的形态
8 ____ 的声响
9 ____ 的气味
10 ____ 的变化
11 ____ 的景观
12 ____ 的清晨
13 ____ 的白天
14 ____ 的黄昏
15 ____ 的夜晚
16 ____ 的色彩
17 ____ 的姿态
18 ____ 的城市
19 ____ 的乡村
20 ____ 的高原
21 ____ 的平地
22 ____ 的瀑布
23 ____ 的浪花
24 ____ 的水汽
25 ____ 的水珠
26 ____ 的隧道
27 ____ 的平台
28 ____ 的梦境
29 ____ 的夜景
30 ____ 的导游
31 ____ 的想象
32 ____ 的现实
33 ____ 的基础
34 ____ 的海报
35 ____ 的消息
36 ____ 的语言
37 ____ 的设计
38 ____ 的时代

二、选词填空 Fill in the blanks with the words provided.

1 同一 ____ 在风、雨、雾、雪中所展现的姿态也各不相同。

    a. 景色　c. 景象
    b. 景观　d. 景物

2 在一天中，清晨、白天、黄昏、夜晚等不同 ____ 给景物涂上了不同的色彩。

    a. 时间　c. 时候
    b. 时段　d. 时代

3 把观察到的景物特征用 ____ 的文字记录下来，就是一篇出色的写景文章。

    a. 生动　c. 活动
    b. 激动　d. 自动

4 开车经过美加边境的水牛城，不久就能望见世界 ____ 的大瀑布了。

    a. 有名   c. 闻名
    b. 出名   d. 知名

5 我们先乘 "雾中少女" 号游船 ____ 瀑布。

    a. 观看   c. 观光
    b. 观察   d. 观赏

6 这时，看到的只是 ____ 的瀑布、飞溅的浪花和弥漫的水汽。

    a. 奔流   c. 奔驰
    b. 奔放   d. 奔跑

7 听到的只是轰鸣的水声和船上游客的 ____ 和欢呼声。

    a. 惊喜   c. 惊险
    b. 惊叫   d. 惊慌

8 ____ 隧道来到突出的平台上，突然发现瀑布就在身旁！

    a. 随着   c. 跟着
    b. 沿着   d. 追着

9 成语 "瓢泼大雨"、"倾盆大雨" 都显得太 ____ 了。

    a. 轻飘   c. 轻便
    b. 轻浮   d. 轻快

10 海报可在公共场所张贴，也可做成电子邮件的附件，通过网络 ____ 。

    a. 传达   c. 传染
    b. 传递   d. 传播

11 设计要新颖 ____ ，才能吸引眼球。

    a. 美丽   c. 美妙
    b. 美观   d. 美好

12 在电子时代，每个人都能自己动手，设计 ____ 的海报。

    a. 优美   c. 鲜美
    b. 完美   d. 精美

三、改错 Correct the errors.

1 同一景物在风、雨、雾、雪中所展现的姿势也各不相同。
2 开车经过美加边境的奶牛城，不久就能望见世界闻名的大瀑布了。
3 远远望去，它像一条白纱，挂在青山绿水之间。
4 奇怪其中的一块瀑布叫 "新娘面纱" 呢。
5 我不禁想起李白写瀑布的名篇："飞流直下三千尺，疑是银河落九天。"
6 暴风雨劈头盖面地打来。
7 在周围三颜六色的聚光灯的照耀下，它显得比白天更多姿多彩。
8 夸张是运用丰富的想象力，在现实的基础上有计划地放大或缩小事物的形象特征，以增强表达效果的修辞手法。

9 嗓子干得直冒火。
10 设计要新颖美观，才能吸引眼睛。

4.7 Phrase training 语句训练

一、造句 Make sentences.

1 重要的是

【课文例句】要写好景，重要的是要仔细观察所写的景物。
【生活例句】你去欧洲旅行，重要的是要去看几个最好的博物馆，比如巴黎的凡尔赛宫。

When you go travelling in Europe, it is important to see some of the best museums, such as the Palace of Versailles in Paris.

2 善于

【课文例句】在观察时，要善于抓住不同季节、不同时间、不同气候、不同地区中景物呈现出的颜色、形态、声响、气味等方面的特征和变化。
【生活例句】刘大山善于讲笑话，所以跟他在一起总是很开心。

Liu Dashan is good at telling jokes, so it's always fun to be with him.

3 难怪

【课文例句】远远望去，它像一匹白纱，挂在青山绿水之间。难怪其中的一块瀑布叫 “新娘面纱” 呢。
【生活例句】林小丽在广州留学了一年，难怪她说汉语带着广东口音呢。

Lin Xiaoli studied in Guangzhou for one year; no wonder she speaks Mandarin with Cantonese accent.

4 不禁

【课文例句】瀑布就在我们面前倾泻下来，我不禁想起中文课上学过的李白写瀑布的名句：“飞流直下三千尺，疑是银河落九天。”
【生活例句】好久没吃妈妈做的中国菜了，小云从大学回家看到一桌好菜，不禁大吃起来。

Xiaoyun had not eaten the Chinese food made by her mom in a long time, so when she came back from college and saw a whole table of delicious dishes, she could not help but eat heartily.

5 只觉得

【课文例句】船开到瀑布前的时候，只觉得天地之间只有瀑布存在，我也已化为其中的一颗水珠了。
【生活例句】江大伟昨晚酒喝多了，现在只觉得头痛想睡觉。

Jiang Dawei drank a lot last night so now he has a headache and is feeling sleepy.

6 不就是

【课文例句】《西游记》中孙悟空的水帘洞不就是这样的吗？
【生活例句】这不就是你一直在找的那本书吗？在你自己的床底下呢。

Is this the book you have always been looking for? It was under your bed!

7 这哪里是……这简直是

【课文例句】这哪里是一瓢水、一盆水呀？这简直是一个巨人把五大湖翻转过来，把水都倒下来了。
【生活例句】妈妈在做一个甜酸鸡，叫东东帮她加点糖，结果东东拿错了瓶子，加了盐。妈妈说："你这哪里是帮忙啊，这简直是添乱么。"

Mom was making sweet and sour chicken and asked Dongdong to help her by adding some sugar. However, Dongdong got the wrong container and added salt. Mom said: "How could you consider this as help? This is simply making trouble!"

8 则是

【课文例句】尼亚加拉瀑布在入夜后则是另一番景象。
【生活例句】文思明跟他妈妈住在南京，他爸爸则是在西安工作，所以他不常见到他爸爸。

Wen Siming lives in Nanjing with his mom, but his dad works in Xi'an, therefore, he does not see his dad very often.

9 特别是

【课文例句】本文用了很多不同的修辞手法，特别是比喻和夸张。
【生活例句】钱春华的记忆力特别好，特别是数字。你告诉她一个电话号码，她马上就记住了。

Qian Chunhua has an excellent memory, especially for numbers. If you tell her a telephone number, she will remember it immediately.

10 一般是

【课文例句】海报一般是用来向群众介绍各种活动（文艺演出、体育比赛、学术报告、社团活动等）的消息。
【生活例句】洛杉矶是四季如春，全年气温一般是在 50 度和80度之间。

It's like spring all year around in Los Angeles. The temperature is usually between 50 and 80 degrees.

11 可……也可

【课文例句】海报可在公共场所张贴，也可做成电子邮件的附件，通过网络传播。
【生活例句】孩子们，我们今天晚上可以去吃中国自助餐，也可以去吃韩国烤肉，你们要去哪儿？

Hey kids, we can go to a Chinese buffet tonight, or we can eat Korean barbeque. Where would you like to go?

二、回答问题 Answer the questions.

1 尼亚加拉大瀑布在哪儿？
2 远远望去，尼亚加拉大瀑布像什么？
3 观赏瀑布的游船叫什么名字？
4 请背诵李白写瀑布的名句。
5 在"雾中少女"号游船上看到的是什么？听到的是什么？
6 怎么才能走到瀑布的后面？

7 请说出两句形容大雨的成语。

8 很多成语中包含有数字。请说出三句。

9 这篇课文从哪四个角度观察、描写大瀑布？

10 为什么说可以把这篇游记当成导游手册？

11 本文用了哪些修辞手法？

12 什么是夸张？

13 海报要写清楚哪些内容？

三、运用夸张手法完成句子Complete the sentences using exaggeration.

1 填空 Fill in the blank with a word chosen from the parentheses.

    a. 我像 ____ 一般飞快地跑回家去。（猴子、兔子）

    b. 你看，这个瓷碗做得多好，它简直比 ____ 还薄。（布、纸）

    c. 我高兴得一蹦三 ____ 高。(尺，米)

    d. 这个包子怎么比 ____ 还硬？能吃吗？（石头、拳头）

2 改写：把下列句子改写成夸张句 Re-write the following sentences, using exaggerations.

    a. 地上都是书，他就坐在地上看书。

    b. 今天天气很冷，你不穿大衣是不能出门的。

    c. 这座山非常高，你怎么爬得上去！

    d. 这家店的东西太贵了，我们走吧。

3 解释以下含有夸张手法的成语 Explain the following idioms that contain exaggerations.

    a. 一步登天

    b. 一毛不拔

    c. 一字千金

    d. 一手遮天

    e. 一掷千金

    f. 三头六臂

    g. 百发百中

    h. 人山人海

    i. 刀山火海

    j. 大海捞针

    k. 顶天立地

    l. 天翻地覆

    m. 飞针走线

    n. 挥汗如雨

    o. 弱不禁风

    p. 光阴似箭

    q. 寸步不离

    r. 罪该万死

4 把下列含有夸张成分的英语习语翻译成中文 Translate the following English idioms, which contain elements of exaggeration, into Chinese.

    a. She eats like a bird.

    b. He worked his fingers to the bone.

c. His father hit the ceiling when he discovered her bad grades.
d. She was really dressed to the teeth at the party.
e. The loud music almost drives me up a wall!

4.8 Composition training 作文训练

一、仿写作文 *Imitative composition*

写一篇游记，要符合以下三个要求：1. 描写一个你去过的美丽的地方，比如一座山或一条河；2. 从不同的角度观察这个地方；3. 用上比喻和夸张。文章的长度不限。

Write a travel journal following three requirements: 1. Describe a beautiful place, such as a mountain or a river that you have visited. 2. Observe this place from different perspectives. 3. Use simile, metaphor, and exaggeration. The length of the article is flexible.

二、情景作文 *Situational composition*

假设你和你的家人正在"雾中少女"号游船上观赏尼亚加拉大瀑布时突然下起了大雨。过了一会儿，雨停日出。请写一篇描写天气、景色和你的心情的短文。

Suppose you and your family were on the "Maid of the Mist" boat enjoying Niagara Falls, when suddenly rain began pouring down. After a while, the heavy storm stopped, and the sun shined again. Please write a short piece about the weather, the scenery and your excitement.

三、串联作文 *Chain story composition*

这个练习是全班同学作为课外作业的集体创作。根据姓名的英文字母的排列，每人依次写一句。文章会放在"黑板"或其他类似的课堂教学管理系统的讨论板上。文章的开端提供在下面。尽量使文章易懂、逻性强辑和生动有趣。尽可能多用夸张手法。你一看到你前面的同学写好了，就应着手写作。一圈下来，轮到的任何人只要觉得故事应该到此为止，就可以结束故事。此后，班上要举行一次讨论。

This will be a collective story created by the whole class as homework. According to the alphabetical order of the class list, each writer is succeeded by the next student. The article will be posted on the discussion board on Blackboard© or a similar learning management system. The beginning of the article is provided below. Try to make the article understandable, logical, and interesting. Use exaggeration to the best of your ability. You should begin to write your sentence as soon as you see the preceding one completed. After the first round, anybody during his or her turn can conclude the story if he or she thinks it's right place to do so. A class discussion of the story will follow.

题目：《大海的怀抱》

今年暑假，我们全家去海边度假。刚把东西搬进度假屋，我们就迫不及待地换上游泳衣，奔到海滩上去了。……

四、进阶作文 *Sequential composition*

以《登山》为题目，写三篇短文。

Write three short pieces in sequence with the title of "Climbing a Mountain".

1   写一个100字左右的段落，描写你的一次登山的经历。山可大可小，但你要
    说明：是哪座山？你在哪一年登上它的？你为什么要登这座 山？

    Write a paragraph of about 100 characters describing your experience climbing a
    mountain. The mountain could be big or small, but you must explain which mountain
    it was, what year you climbed it, and why you climbed this particular mountain.

2   写两个100字左右的段落，描绘这座山的形状、特征。它有什么与众不同的
    地方？从不同的角度观察和描写，并尽量运用夸张手法。

    Write two 100-character paragraphs describing the mountain's shape and other char-
    acteristics. Did it have any unusual aspects? Observe and describe the mountain
    from different perspectives, and to the best of your ability use exaggeration.

3   结合a和b的内容，写一篇500字的游记。要注意仔细观察。

    Combine the contents of the three aforementioned paragraphs and write a 500-char-
    acter travelogue. Pay attention to careful observations.

五、应用文写作 *Practical composition*

中国同学会要举办一个中国新年的庆祝活动，包括演出、游戏和晚餐。请你
制作一张精美的海报。

The Chinese Students Association will hold a Chinese New Year's celebration,
which will include activities such as performances, games, and dinner. Please design
an exquisite poster.

5 第五课　Writing about scenery, part two

绘景篇下

5.1　Writing guide 写作指导

Blending scenery and feelings 情景交融

情景交融是指写作中把景物描写跟人物思想感情紧密结合的艺术手法。景物是客观的，但在不同的人的眼中会有不同的感觉。在同样的环境中，选择什么景物，怎样描写，是因人而异的。在写景的字里行间，自然会渗透作者的感情。

　　元代的马致远(1250–1321)写过一首有名的短诗，叫《秋思》：　"枯藤老树昏鸦，小桥流水人家，古道西风瘦马。夕阳西下，断肠人在天涯。" 句句都是写景，用一组镜头，描绘出秋天傍晚荒郊的景象，是寓情于景。在最后一句中才触景生情，用 "断肠" 两字牵出诗人凄凉的心情来。

Blending scenery with feelings refers to the artistic device that links the description of scenery closely with human thoughts and feelings. The scenery is objective, but different people may have unique feelings when viewing it. In the same environment, what aspects of that environment to choose and how to describe them varies from person to person. It is natural that the author's feelings permeate between the lines of the scenery's description.

Ma Zhiyuan (1250–1321) of the Yuan Dynasty wrote a famous short poem, called "Autumn Thoughts": "Withered vines, old trees, crows in twilight; a small bridge, flowing water, a house; ancient road, west wind, a thin horse. The evening sun is setting to the west; the broken-hearted person is in the remotest corner of the earth." Each line describes scenery; it uses a group of images to depict the scenery of a desolate countryside in the evening, so as to "bestow feelings upon the scenery." Only in the last line, the poet "produces feelings when touching upon the scenery," and uses "heart-broken" to explicitly express his sad mood.

词汇一

1	情景交融		qíngjǐng jiāoróng	(of literary work) fusion of feelings with scenery
2	紧密	緊密	jǐnmì	close together, inseparable
3	客观	客觀	kèguān	objective
4	感觉	感覺	gǎnjué	feeling, sense perception
5	选择	選擇	xuǎnzé	to choose, select
6	因人而异	因人而異	yīnrén éryì	differ from person to person
7	异	異	yì	different
8	字里行间	字裏行間	zìlǐ hángjiān	between the lines
9	自然		zìrán	naturally, of course
10	渗透	滲透	shèntòu	to permeate
11	元代		yuándài	Yuan Dynasty (1271–1368)
12	马致远	馬致遠	mǎzhìyuǎn	poet and play writer (1251–1321)

13	枯		kū	withered
14	藤		téng	vine
15	昏		hūn	dark, dim
16	鸦	鴉	yā	crow
17	夕阳	夕陽	xīyáng	the setting sun
18	夕		xī	sunset
19	断肠	斷腸	duàncháng	heartbroken
20	肠	腸	cháng	intestines
21	天涯		tiānyá	end of the world; remotest place on earth
22	荒郊		huāngjiāo	wilderness, wild countryside
23	寓情于景		yùqíng yújǐng	to imply feelings in a scene
24	寓		yù	to imply, contain
25	触景生情	觸景生情	chùjǐng shēngqíng	to be moved by what one sees
26	牵	牽	qiān	to pull, draw
27	凄凉	淒涼	qīliáng	bleak, desolate; miserable

5.2 Model text 范文

Autumn colors on campus 校园秋色

【提示】秋天是一个引人思考的季节。中国古代的诗人因此常常以秋天为题目写景抒情，如唐朝诗人杜甫（712–770）的《秋兴》和元代诗人马致远（1250–1321）的《秋思》。以《校园秋色》为题作文，要注意情景交融。

Autumn is a season that entices people's thoughts. Because of this, ancient Chinese poets often wrote poems using the word autumn in the title to describe the scenery and express feelings. For example, Du Fu (712–770) of the Tang Dynasty wrote "Autumn Aspirations" and Ma Zhiyuan of the Yuan Dynasty wrote "Autumn Thoughts." Please compose a piece titled "Autumn Colors on Campus," and pay attention to the blending of scenery with feelings.

我们的校园一年四季都很美，但最美的是秋季。
* 点题："校园"和"秋"

九、十月间，周围小山上的树木都染成金色和红色。远远看去，就像一幅绚丽的丝绒，映衬着蓝天白云，让人赞叹大自然的创造力。
* 点题："色"
* 金色1：远山

校园里，草地还是碧绿的，只是点缀着片片金黄色的落叶。风一吹，又一阵树叶飘下来，像一群金色的蝴蝶在空中翻飞。红砖砌成的教学楼前的地上铺了一层落叶，就像一幅油画，使人想起古老的欧洲的大学，令人神往。
* 金色2：校园落叶
* 联想：欧洲老大学

大大小小的花坛都增添了不同的颜色。你看，那边是一大片菊花。有大红的、粉红的，当然最多的是金黄的。中国人用"秋菊傲霜"来赞美它不畏寒冷的品格。
* 金色3：菊花

不但是花草树木，秋天的校园中的生活也是多姿多彩的。学生们经过一个暑假的休整、调节，精力饱满地回到学校，校园也就充满了生机。校园的主要道路上，学生们背着书包，匆匆来去。在钟楼下的大草坪上，有一个班正在上课。学生们围着圈席地而坐，沐浴在金色的秋阳中。
* 金色4：秋阳

如果要为秋天的校园选一个颜色，我会选金色。金色使人想起田野中的麦浪，是丰收的季节。金色使人想起皇冠，是忠诚的象征。但在眼前，金色是铺满道路的落叶，是绽放笑脸的菊花，是柔和宜人的阳光。金色使人感到生命的温暖和人生的充实。
* 结论扣题
* 联想：金色
* 排比：金色

词汇二

1	引		yǐn	to cause, arouse, trigger
2	抒情		shūqíng	to express one's emotion
3	点题	點題	diǎntí	to refer back to the title, bring out the theme
4	周围	周圍	zhōuwéi	surroundings
5	染		rǎn	to dye, tint
6	绚丽	絢麗	xuànlì	bright and colorful, gorgeous
7	丝绒	絲絨	sīróng	velvet
8	映衬	映襯	yìngchèn	to set off, relieve against
9	赞叹	贊歎	zàntàn	to gasp in admiration, praise highly
10	创造力	創造力	chuàngzàolì	creativity
11	碧绿	碧綠	bìlǜ	azure green
12	点缀	點綴	diǎnzhuì	to embellish, intersperse
13	飘	飄	piāo	to flutter, float
14	群		qún	swarm, group
15	蝴蝶		húdié	butterfly
16	翻飞	翻飛	fānfēi	to fly up and down
17	砖	磚	zhuān	brick
18	砌		qì	to lay bricks or stones
19	铺	鋪	pū	to spread, lay, pave
20	令人神往		lìngrén shénwǎng	to cause a craving for, have a strong appeal
21	花坛	花壇	huātán	flower bed, flower terrace
22	增添		zēngtiān	to add, increase
23	菊花		júhuā	chrysanthemum
24	秋菊傲霜		qiūjú àoshuāng	the autumn chrysanthemum braves the frost
25	赞美	贊美	zànměi	to admire, praise
26	畏		wèi	to fear
27	寒冷		hánlěng	chilly, frigid
28	休整		xiūzhěng	rest and reorganization
29	调节	調節	tiáojié	adjustment
30	精力		jīnglì	energy, vigor
31	饱满	飽滿	bǎomǎn	full
32	充满	充滿	chōngmǎn	to be filled with, full of
33	生机	生機	shēngjī	life, vigor, vitality
34	钟楼	鐘樓	zhōnglóu	bell tower, clock tower
35	草坪		cǎopíng	lawn
36	围	圍	wéi	to enclose, surround
37	圈		quān	circle, ring
38	席地而坐		xídì érzuò	to sit on the ground or floor
39	沐浴		mùyù	to bathe, immerse
40	田野		tiányě	field
	麦浪	麥浪	màilàng	waves of wheat, fields of billowing wheat
41	丰收	豐收	fēngshōu	bumper harvest
42	皇冠		huángguān	royal crown
43	忠诚	忠誠	zhōngchéng	loyal, faithful
44	绽放	綻放	zhànfàng	to blossom
45	柔和		róuhé	soft, gentle
46	宜人		yírén	pleasant, delightful
47	充实	充實	chōngshí	rich, substantial

5.3 Commentary 点评

本文紧扣题目，通篇写景，抒情的句子并不多，但作者对校园秋色的赞美之情却充溢在字里行间。

第一段中，"最美的是秋季"直接点题。第二段是对秋天远山的全景描写，并由此引出赞叹。第三段中用了蝴蝶和油画两个比喻，是寓情于景。第四段写菊花，是即景生情。第五段写人，描绘了秋天校园中的一道风景线。在最后一段中，联想和排比的手段加快了文章的节奏，也加重了感情色彩，直至引出最后一句。"金色使人感到生命的温暖和人生的充实，"既丰富了主题，又把情景交融的手段发挥到了极致。

The content of this piece closely relates to its title. It describes the scenery throughout the article without implementing many sentences that directly express the author's feelings. However, the author's admiration for the autumn colors on campus permeates the lines.

In the first paragraph, this sentence: "The most beautiful is autumn," relates directly to the title. The second paragraph is a panoramic description of the remote autumn mountains and the resulting admiration of their beauty. The third paragraph employs two similes – the butterfly and the oil painting – in order "to consign feelings to scenery." The fourth paragraph describes chrysanthemums, which is "to produce feelings upon viewing the scenery." The fifth paragraph depicts people, a unique "scenic sight" on the autumn campus. In the last paragraph, the methods of association and parallelism hasten the article's rhythm, strengthen passion, and lead to the ending sentence. The line, "The golden color makes people feel the warmth of life and the substantiality of life journey" enriches the theme as well as develops the method of "blending feelings with scenery" to its highest level of effectiveness.

词汇三

1	扣		kòu	to button up, buckle, stick to
2	通篇		tōngpiān	throughout the essay
3	充溢		chōngyì	to be full to the brim, be permeated
4	全景		quánjǐng	panorama
5	即景生情		jíjǐng shēngqíng	the scene touches a chord in one's heart
6	风景线	風景線	fēngjǐngxiàn	view, scenic sight
7	联想	聯想	liánxiǎng	association, connection of ideas, feelings, etc.
8	节奏	節奏	jiézòu	rhythm
9	手段		shǒuduàn	method, device
10	发挥	發揮	fāhuī	to bring into play, give free rein to
11	极致	極致	jízhì	perfection, highest attainments

5.4 Rhetoric 修辞

Association 联想

联想是一种心理活动的方式，也是一种重要的文学写作手法。它的特点是从某一事物想到与之有一定联系的另一事物。联想的意义同一个特定的文化传统有着密切的关系。

在中国的诗文中，月亮常能启发人的联想。一钩新月，会让人联想到初生的事物；一轮满月，会让人联想到圆满的生活；月亮的皎洁，又会让人联想到光明磊落的人格。宋朝大诗人苏轼写道："明月几时有？把酒问青天。不知天上宫阙，今夕是何年？"他在中秋之夜，大醉之中，望着明月，联想到了天上的世界和宇宙的永恒，写出千古传诵的佳句。

Association is a type of psychological activity, and also an important literary device. It bridges together two comparable things. The connotation of association is closely related to a certain cultural tradition.

In Chinese poetry and prose, the moon often serves as inspiration to readers, who associate the moon with other ideas. A crescent moon would cause people to relate it to new beginnings, a full moon would make people think about a perfect life, and a lustrous moon would direct people's thoughts to an open and upright character. Su Shi, a great poet of the Song Dynasty wrote: "When did the moon start? I hold a wine cup and ask the blue sky. I don't know that in the palaces in Heaven, what year is it tonight?" While drunk on the night of the Mid-Autumn Festival, looking up at the bright moon, he was led to think about the world of Heaven and the eternal universe, and composed the great poetic lines that have been recited through generations.

词汇四

1	心理		xīnlǐ	psychology, mind
2	某		mǒu	certain, some
3	之		zhī	*used in a place of a person or thing as an object*
4	传统	傳統	chuántǒng	tradition
5	密切		mìqiè	close, intimate
6	关系	關系	guānxì	relation, connection
7	启发	啓發	qǐfā	to inspire, arouse
8	钩	鉤	gōu	hook, *measure word for the crescent moon*
9	初生		chūshēng	nascent, primary
10	轮	輪	lún	wheel, *measure word for the full moon and the sun*
11	圆满	圓滿	yuánmǎn	satisfactory, perfect
12	皎洁	皎潔	jiǎojié	bright and clear
13	光明磊落		guāngmíng lěiluò	frank and forthright
14	人格		réngé	personality, character
15	宋朝		sòngcháo	Song Dynasty (960–1276)
16	苏轼	蘇轼	sūshì	a statesman, poet, and artist (1037–1101)
17	几时	幾時	jǐshí	when, what time
18	把酒		bǎjiǔ	to hold a wine cup
19	宫阙		gōngquè	imperial palace
20	何		hé	what
21	中秋		zhōngqiū	Mid-Autumn Festival
22	宇宙		yǔzhòu	universe, cosmos
23	永恒		yǒnghéng	eternity
24	千古		qiāngǔ	through the ages
25	传诵	傳誦	chuánsòng	to be widely read
26	佳句		jiājù	beautiful line, well-formed sentence

5.5 Practical writing 应用文

Cover letter for a job application 求职信

写求职信要注意以下四个方面。开头要开门见山地写明你对公司有兴趣并想担任他们空缺的职位。第二部分要简短地叙述自己所学的专业以及才能，特别是这些才能将满足公司的需要。没有必要作具体的陈述,详细内容对方可查看你的简历。然后要提供联系方式,并表明你希望迅速得到回音。收尾时要感谢招聘人员阅读你的材料并考虑你的申请。

　　求职信的篇幅不要长,力求简明扼要。态度要诚恳,不需要豪言壮语,也不用华丽的词藻,只要让对方读来觉得亲切、自然、实实在在就行了。

When writing cover letters for job applications, you should pay attention to the following four aspects. In the beginning, you should directly state your interest in the company and your intention to take the open position. In the second part, you should succinctly talk about your major at school and your skills, emphasizing that these skills would meet the need of the company. There is no need to make a full statement – they can find the details in your résumé. Next, you provide contact information, and express that you hope to receive a quick response. At the end, you need to thank the recruiters for reading your materials and considering your application.

The cover letter of a job application should not be long, so you should try to make it succinct. You should be sincere, and you do not need to use heroic words or flowery phrases. It should be sufficient as long as the recruiters feel while reading the cover letter that the applicant is warm, natural, and genuine.

词汇五

1	求职	求職	qiúzhí	to seek a position, apply for a job
2	以下		yǐxià	below, the following
3	开门见山	開門見山	kāimén jiànshān	to be straight to the point, be upfront
4	空缺		kòngquē	vacant position
5	职位	職位	zhíwèi	position, post
6	才能		cáinéng	ability, aptitude, capability
7	满足	滿足	mǎnzú	to satisfy
8	必要		bìyào	necessity
9	陈述	陳述	chénshù	statement
10	对方	對方	duìfāng	other side, opposite side
11	查看		chákàn	to look over, examine
12	简历	簡歷	jiǎnlì	résumé
13	联系	聯繫	liánxì	to contact, connect
14	表明		biǎomíng	to make clear, indicate
15	迅速		xùnsù	quick, rapid, swift
16	回音		huíyīn	reply, response
17	收尾		shōuwěi	closure, ending (of an article, etc.)
18	招聘		zhāopìn	to recruit, invite applications for a job
19	考虑	考慮	kǎolǜ	to consider, deliberate
20	申请	申請	shēnqǐng	application
21	豪言壮语	豪言壯語	háoyán zhuàngyǔ	heroic words
22	华丽	華麗	huálì	resplendent, splendid
23	词藻	詞藻	cízǎo	expressions in literary writings
24	亲切	親切	qīnqiè	warm, close, affectionate

5.6 Vocabulary training 词汇训练

一、填名词 Fill in the blanks with appropriate nouns to form adjective-noun phrases.

1 凄凉的 _____
2 自然的 _____
3 金色的 _____
4 绚丽的 _____
5 碧绿的 _____
6 古老的 _____
7 忠诚的 _____
8 柔和的 _____
9 宜人的 _____
10 温暖的 _____
11 充实的 _____
12 圆满的 _____
13 皎洁的 _____
14 简短的 _____
15 具体的 _____
16 详细的 _____
17 迅速的 _____
18 华丽的 _____
19 亲切的 _____

二、选词填空 Fill in the blanks with the words provided.

1 情景交融指写作中把景物描写跟人物思想感情紧密结合的艺术 ____ 。

    a. 手段   c. 手腕
    b. 手法   d. 手术

2 景物是客观的，但在不同的人的眼中会有不同的 ____ 。

    a. 感情   c. 感受
    b. 感想   d. 感觉

3 秋天是一个引人 ____ 的季节。

    a. 思考   c. 思念
    b. 思想   d. 思辨

4 风一吹，又一阵树叶飘下来，像一 ____ 金色的蝴蝶在空中翻飞。

    a. 组   c. 群
    b. 批   d. 伙

5 红砖 ____ 成的教学楼前的地上铺了一层落叶，就像一幅油画。

    a. 造   c. 砌
    b. 铺   d. 叠

6 中国人用"秋菊傲霜"来赞美它不畏寒冷的 ____ 。

   a. 性格   c. 品格
   b. 风格   d. 资格

7 学生们经过一个暑假的休整、调节，精力饱满地回到学校，校园也就充满了
   ____ 。

   a. 生命   c. 生计
   b. 生活   d. 生机

8 金色使人想起皇冠，是忠诚的 ____ 。

   a. 代表   c. 象征
   b. 表现   d. 比喻

9 金色使人感到生命的温暖和人生的 ____ 。

   a. 充实   c. 诚实
   b. 忠实   d. 结实

10 本文抒情的句子并不多，但作者对校园秋色的赞美之情却 ____ 在字里行间。

   a. 充实   c. 充当
   b. 充足   d. 充溢

11 联想是一种心理活动的 ____ 。

   a. 方式   c. 方向
   b. 方法   d. 方面

12 ____ 朝大诗人苏轼写道："明月几时有？把酒问青天。不知天上宫阙，今夕是何
   年？"

   a. 唐   c. 明
   b. 宋   d. 清

三、改错 Correct the errors.

1 景物是主观的，但在不同的人的眼中会有不同的感觉。
2 唐代的马致远写过一首有名的短诗，叫《秋思》。
3 枯藤老树昏鸦，小桥流水人家，古道东风瘦马。
4 夕阳西下，断肝人在天涯。
5 五句都是写景，用一组镜头，描绘出秋天傍晚荒郊的景象，是寓情于境。
6 远远看去，就像一幅绚丽的丝绸。
7 学生们围着圆席地而坐，沐浴在金色的秋阳中。
8 金色是铺满道路的落叶，是开放笑脸的菊花，是柔和宜人的阳光。
9 "金色使人感到生命的温暖和人生的充实" 既丰富了题目，又把情景交融的手段
   发挥到了极致。
10 月亮的清洁，又会让人联想到光明磊落的人格。
11 然后要提供联系方式，并表明你希望迅速得到回声。
12 写求职信需要用豪言壮语和华丽的词藻。

5.7 **Phrase training** 语句训练

一、用成语造句 Making sentences using the following idioms.

1　触景生情
2　令人神往
3　多姿多彩
4　精力饱满
5　席地而坐
6　光明磊落
7　千古传诵
8　开门见山
9　简明扼要
10　豪言壮语

二、回答问题 Answer the questions.

1　什么是情景交融的写作手法？
2　请背诵马致远的《秋思》。
3　马致远的《秋思》是怎么做到情景交融的？
4　我们的校园哪个季节最美？
5　九、十月间，校园周围小山上的树木都染成了什么颜色？
6　远远看去，周围的小山像什么？
7　秋天的教学楼使人想起什么？
8　校园里有哪些颜色的菊花？
9　中国人用哪句成语来赞美菊花不畏寒冷的品格？
10　为什么秋天的校园充满了生机？
11　为什么学生们在大草坪上围着圈席地而坐？
12　金色使人想起什么？
13　金色使人感到什么？
14　本文第三段中用了哪两个比喻？
15　什么是联想？
16　联想的特点是什么？
17　联想的意义跟什么有密切的关系？
18　在中国的诗文中，什么东西常能启发人的联想？
19　一钩新月会让人联想到什么？
20　一轮满月会让人联想到什么？
21　月亮的皎洁又会让人联想到什么？
22　苏轼在中秋之夜，望着明月，联想到了什么？

三、说明古诗中的联想手法 Explain the use of associations in the following ancient poems.

a　床前明月光，疑是地上霜。举头望明月，低头思故乡。（李白《静夜思》）
b　春眠不觉晓，处处闻啼鸟。夜来风雨声，花落知多少。（孟浩然《春晓》）

5.8 Composition training 作文训练

一、仿写作文 *Imitative composition*

写一篇描写校园的散文，时间应该是除了秋季以外的任何一个季节。要符合以下三个要求：1. 聚焦在几个特别的景色，好像你是用照相机在拍照；2. 即景抒情；3. 用上联想的手法。文章的长度不限。

Write a prose piece about your campus describing its beauty in a season other than autumn. It should adhere to three requirements: 1. Focus on a few uniquely beautiful scenes as if you were using a camera to take pictures. 2. Express your feelings about these scenes. 3. Use association. The length of the article is flexible.

二、情景作文 *Situational composition*

范文中写道：　"在钟楼下的大草坪上，有一个班正在上课。学生们围着圈席地而坐，沐浴在金色的秋阳中。" 假设你是这个班的学生，请写出当时的场景和你的感想。

It is described in the Model Text: "On the big lawn under the Bell Tower, there is a class in session. Students sitting on the grass in a circle are bathed in the golden autumn sun." Suppose you are a student of that class, please elaborate on the situation and your feelings.

三、串联作文 *Chain story composition*

这个练习是全班同学作为课外作业的集体创作。根据姓名的英文字母的排列，每人依次写一句。文章会放在 "黑板" 或其他类似的课堂教学管理系统的讨论板上。文章的开端提供在下面。尽量使文章易懂、逻性强辑和生动有趣。尽可能多用联想的手法。你一看到你前面的同学写好了，就应着手写作。一圈下来，轮到的任何人只要觉得故事应该到此为止，就可以结束故事。此后，班上要举行一次讨论。

This will be a collective story created by the whole class as homework. According to the alphabetical order of the class list, each writer is succeeded by the next student. The article will be posted on the discussion board on Blackboard© or a similar learning management system. The beginning of the article is provided below. Try to make the article understandable, logical, and interesting. Use association to the best of your ability. You should begin to write your sentence as soon as you see the preceding one completed. After the first round, anybody during his or her turn can conclude the story if he or she thinks it's right place to do so. A class discussion of the story will follow.

题目：《夏夜星空》

一个夏天的晚上，我们一家人坐在阳台上乘凉。我们尽情地享受夏夜的凉爽，观看那迷人的星空。星星如宝石般缀满天空......

四、进阶作文 *Sequential composition*

以《雪后》为题，写三篇短文。

Write three short pieces in sequence with the title of "After the Snow."

1   写一个100字左右的段落描写雪景：为什么你那天对雪景特别感兴趣？哪些特点对你特别有吸引力？

Write a paragraph of about 100 characters, describing your observation of a snowy scene. Why were you so interested in the snowy scene that day? What features were most attractive to you?

2   写两个100字左右的段落，进一步从不同的角度描写雪景，并即景抒情。

Write a short piece with two 100-character paragraphs, further describing the snowy scene from different perspectives and expressing your feelings about the scene.

3   结合上述的三个段落的内容，写一个500字的小故事。要注意情景交融。

Combine the contents of the two aforementioned pieces, and write a story of about 500 characters. Pay attention to the blending of scenery and feelings.

五、应用文写作 *Practical composition*

你是一个大学四年级学生。给一个在你的专业范围内的公司写一封求职信。除了在《应用文》写作指导中说到的几点外，你也要讲一下你的中文能力。

You are a college senior. Write a cover letter for a job application to a company in your major field. In addition to the points mentioned in the writing instruction of "Practical Composition," you may also want to talk about your Chinese language ability.

6 第六课　Writing about feelings
抒情篇

6.1 Writing guide 写作指导

情真意美 *True feelings and beautiful expressions*

我们在写人、写事、写景时常要抒发感情。不管是因人抒情或借景抒情，都要讲究真情的流露。

从情感的表达方式上讲，有直接抒情和间接抒情之分。直接抒情比较直白、热烈，多用带有浓重感情色彩的判断句、陈述句等，同时经常会在句中使用感叹词，如"好美啊"、"真想你呀"。间接抒情则比较含蓄。它往往借助叙述、描写和议论等手法来抒发感情。如有名的内蒙古民歌《牧歌》中唱道："蓝蓝的天上白云飘，白云下面马儿跑 . . ."牧民们用草原上的蓝天白云和奔腾的骏马来表达心中的喜悦和赞美之情。

抒情时，应该灵活运用各种表达技巧，如拟人、比喻、对比、排比、象征、联想、夸张等等，才能写得情真意美。

When we write about people, stories or scenery, we often need to express our feelings. Regardless of whether one is expressing feelings for people or scenery, it is important to reveal one's true feelings.

In terms of the way of expressing feelings, there is distinction between direct expression and indirect expression. Direct expression is relatively straightforward and ardent, often using judgmental or declarative sentences with strong and passionate coloring. Also, exclamatory words, such as "how beautiful!" or "I miss you so much!" are often used in the sentences. Indirect expression of feelings is more implicit. It often uses ways such as narration, description, and commenting to express feelings. For example, "A Herdsman's Song," a famous Inner-Mongolian folk song, goes like this: "White clouds are floating on the blue sky; under the white clouds, horses are running . . ." Herdsmen use blue sky, white clouds, and running horses on the grassland to express joy and admiration in their minds.

When expressing feelings, one should skillfully use various devices for expression, such as personification, metaphor, comparison, parallelism, symbolism, association, and exaggeration so as to express true feelings in beautiful terms.

词汇一

1	讲究	講究	jiǎngjiu	to be particular about, to stress
2	流露		liúlù	to reveal, to show unintentionally
3	从 . . . 上讲	從 . . . 上講	cóng . . . shàngjiǎng	to speak in the perspective of
4	直白		zhíbái	straightforward and plain (in speech)

5	热烈	熱烈	rèliè	enthusiastic, ardent
6	浓重	濃重	nóngzhòng	strong, heavy
7	判断	判斷	pànduàn	to judge, determine
8	感叹	感歎	gǎntàn	to sigh with feeling, exclaim
9	感叹词	感歎詞	gǎntàncí	interjection, exclamation
10	含蓄		hánxù	implicit
11	借助		jièzhù	to draw support from
12	议论	議論	yìlùn	comment, discussion
13	内蒙古	内蒙古	nèiměnggǔ	Inner Mongolia
14	牧歌		mùgē	pastoral song
15	奔腾	奔騰	bēnténg	to gallop
16	骏马	駿馬	jùnmǎ	fine horse, steed
17	喜悦	喜悅	xǐyuè	happy, joyous
18	灵活	靈活	línghuó	nimble, flexible
19	技巧		jìqiǎo	technique, skill

6.2 Model text 范文

Musical charm 琴韵

【提示】写一场你听过的音乐会。通过音乐来抒发你的感情。题目中的琴可以是钢琴、小提琴，也可以是胡琴、扬琴，或者别的琴。

Write about a concert you attended. Express your feelings through music. The *qin* in the title can be piano, violin, *huqin* or *yangqin* or other instruments.

今年寒假，我去北京的国家大剧院听了一场音乐会。压台的节目是小提琴协奏曲《梁祝》。我们上学期的中文课上刚学了这个故事，老师也介绍了这个名曲，现在能有机会在这个金碧辉煌的音乐厅里欣赏中国国家交响乐团的演出，我觉得自己激动得快要化成一只蝴蝶了。

- 梁祝

- 激动之情

乐曲开始时，首先由小提琴奏出主题。一共才四句，非常优雅、舒展，使人感到梁山伯与祝英台的绵绵爱意，和他们对幸福生活和美好爱情的向往。这段乐曲很淳朴又富有诗意，仿佛能看到他们在河边漫步、在柳树轻拂的小桥上观鱼、在晚霞映射的窗边读书。这种难分难舍的深沉的爱情拨动着我的心弦。同时，这几句乐曲中也蕴含着曲折，透出一些哀怨，预示着不幸的降临。

- 优雅之情

- 想像：漫步、观鱼、读书
- 深沉之情

大提琴潇洒浑厚的音调随后加入，与独奏小提琴进行着交流对答，描写梁祝二人心心相印的情景。音乐时分时合，如泣如诉，忧伤婉转。突然，音乐急转直下，运用各种乐器和手段，表现出祝父的反对、英台的抗婚、山伯的病逝、以及英台的自尽。小提琴奏出悲愤欲绝、肝肠寸断的音调，描绘出祝英台在梁山伯坟前的"哭坟"情景，造成强烈的悲剧气氛。

- 忧伤之情
- 想像：从抗婚到哭坟
- 悲愤之情

乐曲的最终部份是"化蝶，"梁祝从坟墓中飞出，化为一对蝴蝶，在花间自由飞舞。这时的爱情主题，具有一种轻盈、朦胧和崇高的色彩，既象征一种美妙的梦幻世界，又表达出无限留恋和敬仰的感情。爱情主题的重复演奏，使这种感情不断得到升华。

- 想像：化蝶

- 崇高之情

词汇二

1	琴		qín	general name for certain musical instruments
2	韵	韻	yùn	beautiful or sweet sound, appeal, charm
3	小提琴		xiǎotíqín	violin
4	胡琴		húqín	a two-stringed, bowed instrument
5	扬琴	揚琴	yángqín	dulcimer
6	国家大剧院	國家大劇院	guójiā dà jùyuàn	National Center for the Performing Arts
7	压台	壓台	yātái	grand finale of a theatrical performance, last and the most important item
8	节目	節目	jiémù	program, item on a program
9	奏		zòu	to play, perform (on a musical instrument)
10	协奏曲	協奏曲	xiézòuqǔ	concerto
11	梁祝		liángzhù	Butterfly Lovers (title of a violin concerto)
12	金碧辉煌	金碧輝煌	jīnbì huīhuáng	(of a building, etc.) resplendent and magnificent
13	音乐厅	音樂廳	yīnyuètīng	concert hall
14	欣赏	欣賞	xīnshǎng	to enjoy, appreciate
15	交响乐	交響樂	jiāoxiǎngyuè	symphony
16	优雅	優雅	yōuyǎ	elegant, graceful
17	舒展		shūzhǎn	unfolding and stretching smoothly
18	梁山伯		Liáng Shānbó	personal name
19	祝英台		Zhù Yīngtái	personal name
20	淳朴	淳樸	chúnpǔ	simple and plain
21	富有		fùyǒu	rich in, full of
22	诗意	詩意	shīyì	poetic sentiment
23	仿佛		fǎngfú	as if
24	漫步		mànbù	to stroll, roam
25	柳树	柳樹	liǔshù	willow
26	拂		fú	to stroke, caress
27	晚霞		wǎnxiá	sunset glow, sunset clouds
28	映射		yìngshè	to shine upon
29	舍		shě	to give up, abandon
30	难分难舍	難分難舍	nánfēn nánshě	hard to part with each other
31	深沉	深沈	shēnchén	(of feeling) deep
32	拨	撥	bō	to stir, strike strings
33	心弦		xīnxián	heartstrings
34	蕴含	蘊含	yùnhán	to contain, imply
35	曲折		qūzhé	complication, intricacy
36	哀怨		āiyuàn	sadness
37	预示	預示	yùshì	to foreshow, betoken, indicate
38	不幸		bùxìng	misfortune, bad luck
39	降临	降臨	jiànglín	arrival (written language)
40	潇洒	瀟灑	xiāosǎ	natural and elegant
41	浑厚	渾厚	húnhòu	(of voice) deep and resonant
42	音调	音調	yīndiào	tone
43	随后	隨後	suíhòu	later, subsequently
44	加入		jiārù	to join, take part in
45	交流		jiāoliú	to exchange, interchange
46	对答	對答	duìdá	to answer, respond

47	心心相印		xīnxīn xiāngyìn	to have mutual love and affinity
48	时分时合	時分時合	shífēnshíhé	to separate and join interchangeably
49	泣		qì	to weep, sob
50	如泣如诉	如泣如訴	rúqì rúsù	(of music) very pathetic and touching
51	忧伤	憂傷	yōushāng	distressed
52	婉转	婉轉	wǎnzhuǎn	mild and indirect
53	急转直下	急轉直下	jízhuǎn zhíxià	a sudden turn for the worse
54	乐器	樂器	yuèqì	musical instrument
55	抗婚		kànghūn	to resist an arranged marriage
56	病逝		bìngshì	to die of illness
57	自尽	自盡	zìjìn	to commit suicide
58	悲愤欲绝	悲憤欲絕	bēifèn yùjué	to be torn by grief
59	肝		gān	liver
60	寸		cùn	a unit of length (1/30 meter)
61	肝肠寸断	肝腸寸斷	gāncháng cùnduàn	deeply grieved, heartbroken
62	哭坟	哭墳	kūfén	to mourn (cry) at the tomb
63	坟	墳	fén	grave, tomb
64	悲剧	悲劇	bēijù	tragedy
65	气氛	氣氛	qìfēn	atmosphere
66	最终	最終	zuìzhōng	finally, ultimately
67	坟墓	墳墓	fénmù	grave, tomb
68	轻盈	輕盈	qīngyíng	lighthearted and melodious
69	朦胧		ménglóng	misty, obscure
70	崇高		chónggāo	sublime, lofty
71	美妙		měimiào	wonderful, beautiful
72	梦幻	夢幻	mènghuàn	dream, fantasy
73	留恋	留戀	liúliàn	(of feeling) lingering, attached
74	敬仰		jìngyǎng	to revere, venerate
75	重复	重複	chóngfù	to repeat, duplicate
76	升华	升華	shēnghuá	sublimation

6.3 Commentary 点评

抒情是音乐的一个主要功能，欣赏音乐就是要把自己沉浸在音乐中，体会它的感情。《梁祝》是个标题音乐，又是叙事性的，所以本文就顺着乐曲（也是故事）的发展，抒发自己的感受。作者的感情随着音乐起伏，从优雅、忧伤、悲愤到崇高，表达得真挚、感人。

欣赏音乐和表达感情都要运用丰富的想象力。在开始听到乐曲的主题时，作者仿佛看到了梁祝在漫步、在观鱼、在读书。随着音乐的发展，又仿佛看到英台从抗婚到哭坟的不同场景。想像力极大地帮助了作者对音乐的理解和感情的抒发。

Expressing feelings is one of the major functions of music. Appreciating music means to immerse yourself in the music to experience its emotion. "The Butterfly Lovers" is a musical piece and is in narrative style, so this article evolves along the development of the music (as well as the story) and expresses the author's feelings. The author's emotion follows the modulation of music, from graceful, melancholy, grievous to sublime, all of which are expressed genuinely and powerfully.

Both appreciating music and expressing feelings needs to utilize rich imagination. In the beginning when hearing the theme of the music, the author seems to see Liang Shanbo and Zhu Yingtai strolling, watching fish and reading. Along the development of the music, again, the author seems to see different scenes of Yingtai from "Resisting the marriage" to "Crying at the Tomb." Imagination helps the author's understanding of the music and the expression of his or her feelings to a great degree.

词汇三

1	沉浸	沈浸	chénjìn	to be immersed in
2	标题音乐	標題音樂	biāotí yīnyuè	program music
3	顺	順	shùn	along with, in the same direction
4	起伏		qǐfú	rise and fall
5	真挚	真摯	zhēnzhì	sincere, genuine

6.4 Rhetoric 修辞

Imagination 想像

想象是文学写作的重要手段。想像出来的内容比较丰富，一般都有具体的形象化的情景描写。这些情景是眼前看不到却又合情合理的。

例如在安徒生童话《卖火柴的小女孩》中，小女孩在快要冻死的时候擦亮了火柴，作者赋予她丰富的想象：点燃第一根火柴，觉得自己好像坐在一个大火炉前；第二根，仿佛看见了正冒着香气的烤鹅；第三根，觉得自己坐在一棵圣诞树下；第四根，仿佛看见了奶奶；最后点燃了一大把火柴，奶奶把她抱在怀里带走了。这些想象使读者格外同情这个小女孩。不仅如此，作者还借助想象，提出了穷苦孩子的理想：一个 "没有寒冷、没有饥饿，没有焦虑" 的地方。

Imagination is an important device for literary writing. The imagined content is relatively rich, and usually contains detailed and lively descriptions of scenes. These scenes cannot be seen physically, but they are reasonable.

For example, in Hans Christian Anderson's "The Little Match Girl," the girl, before she is frozen to death, lights matches, and the author endows her with a rich imagination. When she lights the first match, she feels as if she is sitting by a large stove. With the second match, she sees an aromatic roasted goose. The third match makes her feel like she is sitting under a Christmas tree. With the fourth one, she sees her grandma as an illusion. At last, she lights a bundle of matches, and her grandma takes her away in her arms. Her imagination makes readers especially sympathize with the little girl. Furthermore, by using imagination, the author also projects the ideal home for poor children – a place with "neither cold, nor hunger, nor anxiety."

词汇四

1	安徒生		āntúshēng	Hans Christian Andersen (1805–1875), a Danish writer
2	童话	童話	tónghuà	children's story, fairy tale
3	冻死	凍死	dòngsǐ	to freeze to death
4	擦		cā	to strike (a match)
5	赋予	賦予	fùyǔ	to endow, give
6	点燃	點燃	diǎnrán	to light, kindle, ignite
7	火炉	火爐	huǒlú	(heating) stove, fireplace
8	烤鹅	烤鵝	kǎo'é	roasted goose
9	圣诞树	聖誕樹	shèngdàn shù	Christmas tree

10	圣	聖	shèng	sage, saint, holy
11	诞（生）	誕（生）	dàn(shēng)	birth
12	格外		géwài	especially, particularly
13	同情		tóngqíng	to sympathize
14	不仅	不僅	bùjǐn	not only
15	提出		tíchū	to put forward, set forth, propose
16	饥饿	饑餓	jī'è	hunger, starvation
17	焦虑	焦慮	jiāolǜ	anxiety

6.5 Practical writing 应用文

Résumé 简历

简历要"简"：内容要简要，语言要简洁。

在内容上，要用表格的形式列出自己的主要经历，让招聘人员一目了然。应根据企业和职位的要求，巧妙突出自己的优势，给人留下鲜明深刻的印象。短短一份"成就记录,"远胜于长长的"工作经验"。

语言要朴素、准确，多用短句。尽量用客观的陈述，一般不应该出现 "我" 的字样。这里是不需要描写、抒情、议论的，也不要用任何文学手法。

此外，要根据你的目的，突出重点。是申请工作还是申请读研究院？在材料编排上要有所不同。

A résumé should be brief: the content needs to be concise, and the language needs to be succinct.

As far as content is concerned, one needs to list his or her main experiences in the form of a table in order to enable the recruiters to read it over in a glance. Based on a company's given information and the requirements for the position, you should prudently emphasize your strengths, leaving a fresh and deep impression on people. A short list of "achievement records" is far better than a long list of "work experience."

The language should be straightforward and accurate, using many short sentences. Try to make objective statements. Usually, the word "I" should not appear. There is no need for description, expression of feelings or discussion. Do not use any literary devices.

In addition, based on your purpose, make the key points stand out. Are you applying for a job or for graduate schools? Respective materials should be arranged differently.

词汇五

1	简要	簡要	jiǎnyào	concise
2	简洁	簡潔	jiǎnjié	terse, succinct
3	表格		biǎogé	form, table
4	列		liè	to list
5	目		mù	眼睛，看 to see
6	一目了然		yīmù liǎorán	to see clearly at a glance
7	应	應	yīng	应该 should
8	企业	企業	qǐyè	enterprise, business
9	优势	優勢	yōushì	advantage, strength, superiority
10	成就		chéngjiù	accomplishment, achievement
11	记录	記錄	jìlù	record, notes
12	胜	勝	shèng	to surpass, be better than
13	朴素	樸素	pǔsù	simple, plain

14	尽量	盡量	jǐnliàng	to the best of one's ability, as far as possible
15	字样	字樣	zìyàng	word, expression
16	研究院		yánjiūyuàn	research institute, graduate school
17	编排		biānpái	to arrange
18	有所不同		yǒusuǒ bùtóng	有点不一样 slightly different

6.6 Vocabulary training 词汇训练

一、填名词 Fill in the blanks with appropriate nouns to form adjective-noun phrases.

1 直白的 ＿＿＿＿
2 热烈的 ＿＿＿＿
3 浓重的 ＿＿＿＿
4 奔腾的 ＿＿＿＿
5 灵活的 ＿＿＿＿
6 激动的 ＿＿＿＿
7 优雅的 ＿＿＿＿
8 舒展的 ＿＿＿＿
9 幸福的 ＿＿＿＿
10 美好的 ＿＿＿＿
11 淳朴的 ＿＿＿＿
12 深沉的 ＿＿＿＿
13 曲折的 ＿＿＿＿
14 哀怨的 ＿＿＿＿
15 不幸的 ＿＿＿＿
16 潇洒的 ＿＿＿＿
17 浑厚的 ＿＿＿＿
18 忧伤的 ＿＿＿＿
19 婉转的 ＿＿＿＿
20 悲愤的 ＿＿＿＿
21 强烈的 ＿＿＿＿
22 自由的 ＿＿＿＿
23 轻盈的 ＿＿＿＿
24 朦胧的 ＿＿＿＿
25 崇高的 ＿＿＿＿
26 美妙的 ＿＿＿＿
27 无限的 ＿＿＿＿
28 重复的 ＿＿＿＿
29 主要的 ＿＿＿＿
30 真挚的 ＿＿＿＿
31 感人的 ＿＿＿＿
32 丰富的 ＿＿＿＿
33 寒冷的 ＿＿＿＿
34 饥饿的 ＿＿＿＿
35 痛苦的 ＿＿＿＿

36 简要的 ____
37 简洁的 ____
38 巧妙的____
39 鲜明的 ____
40 深刻的 ____
41 朴素的 ____
42 准确的 ____

二、选词填空 Fill in the blanks with the words provided.

1 直接抒情比较直白、热烈，多用带有 ____ 感情色彩的判断句、陈述句等.

    a. 深重   c. 贵重
    b. 严重   d. 浓重

2 间接抒情则比较含蓄。它往往 ____ 叙述、描写和议论等手法来抒发感情。

    a. 借用   c. 借助
    b. 借鉴   d. 借问

3 牧民们用草原上的蓝天白云和 ____ 的骏马来表达心中的喜悦和赞美之情。

    a. 奔忙   c. 奔跑
    b. 奔腾   d. 奔走

4 抒情时，应该灵活运用各种表达 ____ ，如拟人、比喻、排比、象征、联想、夸张等等。

    a. 技术   c. 技艺
    b. 技巧   d. 技法

5 压台的节目是 ____ 协奏曲《梁祝》。

    a. 小提琴 c. 钢琴
    b. 大提琴 d. 扬琴

6 乐曲开始时，首先由小提琴奏出主题。一共才四句，非常优雅、____ 。

    a. 舒服   c. 舒展
    b. 舒适   d. 舒畅

7 这种难分难舍的 ____ 的爱情拨动着我的心弦。

    a. 深沉   c. 深入
    b. 深刻   d. 深远

8 大提琴潇洒浑厚的音调随后加入，与独奏小提琴进行着 ____ 对答。

    a. 交通   c. 交往
    b. 交际   d. 交流

9 小提琴奏出悲愤欲绝的音调，描绘出祝英台在梁山伯坟前的"哭坟"情景，造成 ____ 的悲剧气氛。

    a. 强大   c. 强烈
    b. 强壮   d. 强硬

10 抒情是音乐的一个主要 ____ 。

    a. 功课   c. 功劳
    b. 功夫   d. 功能

11 欣赏音乐和表达感情都要运用丰富的 ____ 力。

    a. 观察   c. 想像
    b. 注意   d. 判断

12 最后点燃了一大 ____ 火柴，奶奶把她抱在怀里带走了。

    a. 根   c. 串
    b. 把   d. 盒

13 这些想象使读者 ____ 同情这个小女孩。

    a. 格外   c. 此外
    b. 例外   d. 另外

14 不仅如此，作者还借助想象，提出了穷苦孩子的 ____ 。

    a. 思想   c. 联想
    b. 感想   d. 理想

15 简历要"简"：内容要简要，语言要 ____ 。

    a. 简洁   c. 简便
    b. 简要   d. 简朴

16 要用表格的 ____ 列出自己的主要经历，让招聘人员一目了然。

    a. 形状   c. 形式
    b. 形象   d. 形态

三、改错 Correct the errors.

1 不管是因人抒情或借景抒情，都要讲究真情的暴露。
2 乐曲开始时，首先由小提琴奏出标题。
3 这段乐曲很淳朴又富有歌意。
4 仿佛能看到他们在晚霞影射的窗边读书。
5 这种难分难舍的深沉的爱情拨动着我的琴弦。
6 这几句乐曲中也蕴含着曲折，透出一些哀怨，表示着不幸的降临。
7 大提琴潇洒浑厚的声调随后加入，与独奏小提琴进行着交流对答。
8 梁祝从坟墓中飞出，化为一对蜜蜂，在花间自由飞舞。
9 这时的爱情主题，具有一种轻盈、朦胧和崇高的颜色。
10 爱情主题的重复演奏，使这种感情不断得到提高。
11 欣赏音乐就是要把自己沉没在音乐中，体会它的感情。
12 本文沿着乐曲的发展，抒发自己的感受。
13 作者的感情随着音乐起伏，表达得真挚、感动。
14 卖火柴的小姑娘仿佛看见了正冒着香气的烤鸭。
15 短短一份"成功记录"远胜于长长的"工作经验"。
16 写简历的语言要朴素、准确，多用长句。
17 写简历也需要运用描写、抒情、议论等文学手法。

6.7 Phrase training 语句训练

一、用句型造句 Make sentences using the following sentence patterns.

1 不管 . . . . . . 都要

【课文例句】不管是因人抒情或借景抒情，都要讲究真情的流露。

【生活例句】不管你去黄石公园或优胜美地，你都要带上你的高级相机，那里的好镜头太多了。

No matter whether you go to Yellowstone or Yosemite, you should take your advanced camera with you – there are too many beautiful scenes.

2 从 . . . . . . 上讲

【课文例句】从情感的表达方式上讲，有直接抒情和间接抒情之分。

【生活例句】从环境上讲，我觉得住在小城市比大城市好，因为那儿空气好，也很安静。

In terms of the environment, I think living in a small town is better than living in a big city because the air quality is good, and it's also very quiet there.

3 用 . . . . . . 来

【课文例句】牧民们用草原上的蓝天白云和奔腾的骏马来表达心中的喜悦和赞美之情。

【生活例句】我每天早上六点用闹钟来叫醒我，起床后就去健身房锻炼。

I use an alarm to wake up at 6:00 every morning. After I get up, I go to the gym to work out.

4 应该 . . . . . . 才能

【课文例句】抒情时，应该灵活运用各种表达技巧，如拟人、比喻、对比、象征、联想、夸张等等，才能写得情真意美。

【生活例句】你想考医学院吗？你应该先把生物学、化学、物理学、社会学等功课都好好复习一下，才能去参加考试。

Do you want to apply for medical school? You should have a good review of biology, chemistry, physics, and sociology before taking the exams.

5 （激动）得 . . . . . .

【课文例句】现在能有机会在这个金碧辉煌的音乐厅里欣赏中国国家交响乐团的演出，我觉得自己激动得快要化成一只蝴蝶了。

【生活例句】爸爸说我们今年暑假去中国旅行，我听了高兴得跳了起来。

Dad said that we will go travel around China this summer. Having heard this, I was so happy that I jumped into the air.

6 既 . . . . . . 又

【课文例句】这时的爱情主题，具有一种轻盈、朦胧和崇高的色彩，既象征一种美妙的梦幻世界，又表达出无限留恋和敬仰的感情。

【生活例句】登山既能锻炼身体，又能欣赏自然风景，我们一起去登山吧。

Climbing mountains is good exercise, and we can also enjoy the natural scenery. Let's go climb a mountain!

7   ……不仅如此……

【课文例句】这些想象使读者格外同情这个小女孩。不仅如此，作者还借助想象，提出了穷苦孩子的理想：一个"没有寒冷、没有饥饿，没有痛苦的地方"。
【生活例句】昨天的中文考试我考得不太好。二十道题目，有十五道答错了，不仅如此，还有五道没来得及做。

I didn't do very well on the Chinese exam yesterday. There were 20 questions, and I gave wrong answers to 15 of them. In addition, I didn't have time to do the other five.

8   在……上

【课文例句】在内容上，要用表格的形式列出自己的主要经历，让招聘人员一目了然。
【生活例句】王平在饮食上很讲究，他不吃白面包，说那没有营养。

Wang Ping is very picky about food. He does not eat white bread, claiming that it does not have nutritional value.

9   有所……

【课文例句】是申请工作还是申请读研究院？在材料编排上要有所不同。
【生活例句】关于李丽芬离婚的事你有所不知，原因是她先生有了小三，所以你不能怪她。

You don't know much about Li Lifen's divorce. The reason for it is that her husband has a mistress. Therefore, you should not blame her.

二、回答问题 Answer the questions.

1   不管是因人抒情或借景抒情，都要讲究什么？
2   从情感的表达方式上讲，有哪两种抒情？
3   直接抒情时，经常会用什么样的句子？
4   间接抒情时，往往借助什么手法来抒发感情？
5   《牧歌》是什么地方的民歌？
6   抒情时，怎样才能写得情真意美？
7   今年寒假，"我"在哪儿听了一场音乐会？
8   压台的节目是什么？
9   小提琴奏出的主题使人感到什么？
10 听着这段淳朴而又富有诗意乐曲，仿佛能看到什么？
11 为什么说这几句乐曲也预示着不幸的降临？
12 这个乐曲运用各种乐器和手段表现了哪些场面？
13 乐曲的最终部份是什么？
14 在安徒生童话《卖火柴的小女孩》中，小女孩在快要冻死的时候擦亮了几根火柴？
15 在点燃每根火柴时，小女孩看到了什么？
16 安徒生提出的穷苦孩子的理想是什么？
17 怎么才能让招聘人员在看简历时，对自己的主要经历一目了然？
18 写简历要用什么样的语言？

三、用抒情词汇造句 Make sentences using words that express feelings.

1　请写出十个表示好心情的形容词，并选其中五个造句。
2　请写出十个表示坏心情的形容词，并选其中五个造句。

6.8 Composition training 作文训练

一、仿写作文 *Imitative composition*

写一篇关于一个激发出你的丰富感情的活动的文章，要符合以下两个要求：1. 根据对这个活动的观察抒发感情；2. 运用不同的文学手段，如拟人、比喻、对比、排比、象征、联想和想象等。文章的长度不限。

Write an article about an experience that inspired rich feelings and excitement, following two requirements: 1. Express feelings through observation of the events. 2. Use different literary devices such as personification, metaphor, contrast, parallelism, symbolism, association, and imagination. The length of the article is flexible.

二、情景作文 *Situational composition*

听一下《梁祝》小提琴协奏曲，再写下你的印象。充分运用想象。

Listen to the violin concerto "The Butterfly Lovers" and write about your impressions. Use your imagination to a great extent.

三、串联作文 *Chain story composition*

这个练习是全班同学作为课外作业的集体创作。根据姓名的英文字母的排列，每人依次写一句。文章会放在"黑板"或其他类似的课堂教学管理系统的讨论板上。文章的开端提供在下面。尽量使文章易懂、逻辑性强和生动有趣。尽可能多用想象。你一看到你前面的同学写好了，就应着手写作。一圈下来，轮到的任何人只要觉得故事应该到此为止，就可以结束故事。此后，班上要举行一次讨论。

This will be a collective story created by the whole class as homework. According to the alphabetical order of the class list, each writer is succeeded by the next student. The article will be posted on the discussion board on Blackboard©. The beginning of the article is provided below. Try to make the article understandable, logical, and interesting. Use imagination to the best of your ability. You should begin to write your sentence as soon as you see the preceding one completed. After the first round, anybody during his or her turn can conclude the story if he or she thinks it's right place to do so. A class discussion of the story will follow.

题目："二十年后回母校"

光阴似箭，一眨眼，我大学毕业已经二十年了。今年六月一日是我们年级的商学院的团聚日。我坐了一天的飞机赶回母校。在飞机上就在想：学校会有很大的变化吧？同学还认得出来吗？……

四、进阶作文 *Sequential composition*

以《五月 – 离别的季节》为题，写三篇短文。

Write three short pieces in sequence with the title of "May: A Season for Separation."

1   写一个100字左右的段落，交代五月是个离别的季节。毕业的同学向师长和同学告别，离开校园，走向社会。没毕业的也要三个月后再见面。

Write a paragraph of about 100 characters, explaining how May is a season for separation. Those who graduate say farewell to teachers and students before leaving the campus and walking forward to join society. Those who are not graduating also would not see each other until after three months.

2   写两个100字左右的段落。每段写一个事件、人物、场面或景色，来抒发你的离别之情。充分发挥你的想象力。

Write two 100-character paragraphs. In each paragraph, write about an event, a person or a scene in order to express your feelings about separation. Use your imagination to a great extent.

3   结合a和b的内容，写一篇500字的抒情短文。

Combine the contents of the aforementioned two pieces, and write a short piece of 500 characters to express your feelings.

五、应用文写作 *Practical composition*

写一份自己的中文简历，目的要明确：申请实习、工作或读研究所。

Write a résumé of your own in Chinese. The goal should be clear: you should apply for an internship, a job or graduate school.

7 第七课　Persuasive writing
议论篇

7.1　Writing guide 写作指导

Three methods of argumentation 论证三法

议论文有三个要素：论点、论据和论证。论点要明确，论据要充分，论证要严密。

常用的论证方法有下列几种。首先是归纳法，即用几个平行的分论点来支持中心论点，以显示思维的全面性。如《梅花香自苦寒来》可以分解为这三个分论点：1、苦可以激发进取心；2、苦可以培养坚强的意志；3、苦可以启发创造精神。

其次是演绎法，即对事理作纵深剖析，以显示思维的深刻性。如《在困难面前》可以分解成这样的几个分论点：1、要承认困难；2、要不怕困难；3、要战胜困难。

最后是比较法，即从成正反两个方面表达观点，以显示思维的鲜明性。如《学贵多问》可以分解成这两个分论点：1、多问可以促进讨论，便于释疑；2、少问导致孤陋寡闻，易于犯错。

There are three major elements for writing a persuasive essay: arguments, supporting evidence, and argumentation. Arguments should be clearly defined, supporting evidence should be substantial, and argumentation should be firmly constructed.

Common strategies for argumentation are as follows. The first is induction, which is to use a few paralleled sub-arguments to support the central argument in order to show the inclusiveness of thinking. For example, the main argument of "The Fragrance of Plum Blossoms Are from Bitter Cold" can be broken up into the following three sub-arguments: 1. Bitterness can stimulate an enterprising spirit. 2. Bitterness can foster a strong will. 3. Bitterness can inspire innovation.

The second strategy is deduction, which is to perform deep analyses in order to show the profundity of thinking. For example, the essay "Facing Difficulties" can be broken up into these sub-arguments: 1. One needs to acknowledge difficulties. 2. One should not be afraid of difficulties. 3. One has to overcome difficulties.

The last strategy is comparison, which is to express views from both affirmative and opposing perspectives in order to show the distinctiveness of thinking. For example, the main point of "Asking Questions Is Valuable for Learning" can be broken up into two sub-arguments: 1. Asking many questions can facilitate discussion and clear up doubts. 2. Asking fewer questions may lead to isolation from information and lead to easily making mistakes.

词汇一

1	论证	論證	lùnzhèng	argumentation, demonstration
2	议论文	議論文	yìlùnwén	persuasive writing
3	论点	論點	lùndiǎn	argument, thesis, point of view
4	论据	論據	lùnjù	grounds of argument, supporting material
5	严密	嚴密	yánmì	accurate, tight, well-knit
6	下列		xiàliè	listed or mentioned below, following
7	归纳	歸納	guīnà	induction
8	即		jí	就是, namely
9	平行		píngxíng	parallel
10	分		fēn	subordinate
11	支持		zhīchí	to support
12	显示	顯示	xiǎnshì	to show, demonstrate
13	思维	思維	sīwéi	thinking, thought
14	梅花		méihuā	plum blossom
15	自		zì	从 from
16	苦寒		kǔhán	bitter cold
17	分解		fēnjiě	to separate into parts, break up
18	为	爲	wéi	成 to
19	激发	激發	jīfā	to inspire, arouse, stimulate
20	进取心	進取心	jìnqǔxīn	enterprising spirit, desire to advance
21	培养	培養	péiyǎng	to foster, train, cultivate
22	坚强	堅強	jiānqiáng	strong, firm
23	意志		yìzhì	will
24	创造	創造	chuàngzào	to create, produce
25	演绎	演繹	yǎnyì	deduction, inference
26	事理		shìlǐ	reason, logic
27	纵深	縱深	zòngshēn	depth, deep
28	剖析		pōuxī	to analyze, dissect
29	承认	承認	chéngrèn	to admit, acknowledge
30	战胜	戰勝	zhànshèng	to overcome, conquer
31	正反		zhèngfǎn	affirmative and opposing
32	贵	貴	guì	valuable, precious, important
33	释疑	釋疑	shìyí	to clear up doubts, answer questions
34	导致	導致	dǎozhì	to cause, result in
35	孤陋寡闻	孤陋寡聞	gūlòu guǎwén	ignorant and ill-informed

7.2 Model text 范文

Confidence and conceit 自信与自负

【提示】选用论证三法（归纳、演绎、比较）中的一个方法写一篇议论文。自己命题。注意论点要明确、论据要充分、论证要严密。

Choose one of the three strategies of argumentation (induction, deduction, and comparison) and write a persuasive essay. Make a title by yourself. Please be aware that your argument should be well-defined, supporting materials should be substantial, and argumentation should be firmly constructed.

自信与自负有什么区别呢？自信与自负字面上仅一字之差。初看起来，自信的人与自负的人都对自我高度肯定，对自己的能力充满信心。两者的差别往往是细微的，但实际上也是巨大的，并且是可以辨别的。

一个人的自信是基于对自己的能力的充分而正确的了解。著名交响乐指挥家小泽征尔，年轻时参加一次国际指挥家大赛。他按照评委会给的乐谱指挥演奏，敏锐地发现了不和谐的声音，就觉得乐谱有问题。但是，评委会的权威人士坚持说乐谱绝对没问题，是他错了。面对一大批音乐大师，他坚定地说："不！一定是乐谱错了！"话音刚落，评委们立即站起来，热烈鼓掌，祝贺他大赛夺魁。原来，这是评委们精心设计的"圈套"，以此来检验指挥家的能力。小泽征尔因充满自信而摘取了世界指挥家大赛的桂冠。所以说，自信是一个人事业成功的保证。

自负的人，是对自己取得的成绩和聪明程度过分自信。法兰西第一帝国的缔造者拿破仑是个军事天才。有一次他在过阿尔卑斯山时说"我比阿尔卑斯山还要高！"的确，他一度征服大半个欧洲，但他的自负使他无限制的扩张，最后在滑铁卢惨败，被流放到大西洋的一个岛上。自视太高、轻视对手往往导致自负者的失败。

俗话说："人贵有自知之明"。自知之明不正是自信与自负的分界线吗？自负的实质是无知，是对自己和他人的能力缺乏正确的评估。那么，怎样区分自信与自负呢？自负的人往往狂妄自大、目空一切，说的比做的多，又只想听好话。自信的人却充满活力又谦虚谨慎，一步一个脚印地往前走。你要做哪一种人呢？

- 以问句开篇
- 中心论点
- 正面论述：自信
- 论据：小泽征尔
- 反面论述：自负
- 论据：拿破仑
- 反问句
- 分界线：自知之明
- 问句
- 识别方法
- 以问句结束

词汇二

1	自信		zìxìn	self-confidence
2	自负	自負	zìfù	conceit
3	区别	區別	qūbié	difference
4	字面		zìmiàn	literal
5	仅	僅	jǐn	只, just, only
6	差		chā	difference
7	自我		zìwǒ	self
8	高度		gāodù	highly
9	肯定		kěndìng	affirmation
10	信心		xìnxīn	confidence
11	两者	兩者	liǎngzhě	the two sides
12	差别		chābié	difference, disparity
13	巨大		jùdà	huge, enormous
14	并且	並且	bìngqiě	and, also
15	辨别		biànbié	to distinguish, differentiate
16	基于		jīyú	based on, on account of
17	著名		zhùmíng	famous, well-known
18	指挥	指揮	zhǐhuī	(music) conductor
19	小泽征尔	小澤征爾	xiǎozé zhēng'ěr	Seiji Ozawa (b. 1935), a Japanese-American conductor
20	评委会	評委會	píngwěihuì	panel of judges
21	乐谱	樂譜	yuèpǔ	music score, sheet music, music
22	演奏		yǎnzòu	to play a musical instrument
23	敏锐	敏銳	mǐnruì	acute, keen

24	和谐	和諧	héxié	harmonious
25	权威人士	權威人士	quánwēi rénshì	authoritative people
26	坚持	堅持	jiānchí	to persist in, insist on
27	绝对	絕對	juéduì	absolutely, definitely
28	面对	面對	miànduì	to face, confront
29	批		pī	group
30	大师	大師	dàshī	master
31	坚定	堅定	jiāndìng	firm, resolute
32	话音	話音	huàyīn	one's voice in speech
33	落		luò	to drop, fall
34	评委	評委	píngwěi	judge, member of a panel of judges
35	鼓		gǔ	drum, to strike or play a music instrument
36	掌		zhǎng	palm
37	鼓掌		gǔzhǎng	to applaud
38	夺魁	奪魁	duókuí	to come first, win first prize, win the championship
39	夺	奪	duó	to take by force, seize, wrest
40	魁		kuí	chief, head
41	原来	原來	yuánlái	as it turns out
42	精心		jīngxīn	painstakingly, elaborately
43	圈套		quāntào	trap, snare
44	检验	檢驗	jiǎnyàn	to test, examine, inspect
45	摘取		zhāiqǔ	to pick, pluck
46	桂		guì	cassia, laurel
47	冠		guān	帽子, hat
48	桂冠		guìguān	laurels
49	保证	保證	bǎozhèng	guarantee
50	程度		chéngdù	level, degree
51	过分	過分	guòfèn	excessive, extreme
52	法兰西	法蘭西	Fǎlánxī	France
53	帝国	帝國	dìguó	empire
54	缔造者	締造者	dìzào zhě	founder
55	拿破仑	拿破侖	Nápòlún	Napoleon Bonaparte (1769–1821)
56	军事	軍事	jūnshì	military affairs
57	天才		tiāncái	genius, talent
58	阿尔卑斯	阿爾卑斯	A'ěrbēisī	Alps
59	一度		yīdù	once, at one time
60	征服		zhēngfú	to conquer
61	限制		xiànzhì	restriction, limit
62	扩张	擴張	kuòzhāng	to expand
63	滑铁卢	滑鐵盧	Huátiělú	Waterloo (a town in Belgium where Napoleon was defeated in 1815)
64	战役	戰役	zhànyì	battle
65	惨败	慘敗	cǎnbài	disastrous defeat
66	流放		liúfàng	to exile, banish
67	大西洋		Dàxīyáng	Atlantic Ocean
68	岛	島	dǎo	island
69	自视	自視	zìshì	to consider or think oneself
70	轻视	輕視	qīngshì	to despise, look down
71	对手	對手	duìshǒu	opponent, rival
72	正		zhèng	just, right, exactly
73	分界线	分界線	fēnjièxiàn	line of demarcation, boundary
74	实质	實質	shízhì	substance, essence
75	无知	無知	wúzhī	ignorance
76	缺乏		quēfá	to be short of, lack
77	评估	評估	pínggū	evaluation, estimate
78	区分	區分	qūfēn	to differentiate, distinguish

79	狂妄		kuángwàng	wildly arrogant, extremely conceited
80	自大		zìdà	self-important, arrogant
81	一切		yīqiè	all, every
82	目空一切		mùkōng yīqiè	to look down on everyone else, be extremely arrogant
83	活力		huólì	energy, vigor
84	谦虚	謙虛	qiānxū	modest, humble
85	谨慎	謹慎	jǐnshèn	prudent, circumspect
86	脚印	腳印	jiǎoyìn	footprint

7.3 Commentary 点评

本文是一篇用比较法写的议论文，对照的两个方面在题目中已点明了。文中用了两个真实的故事作为论据，非常贴切、有力。

中国古诗作法有 “起承转合”一说，一篇议论文也常常是由这四部分构成的。本文的四个自然段落正是发挥了这四个功能。第一段是起，提出论点。第二段是承，接着说明正面的观点。第三段是转，批驳反面论点。第四段是合，得出结论。由于结构完整，层次清楚，读来气势充沛，令人信服。

This persuasive essay was written using the strategy of comparison. The two contrasting sides are pointed out in the title. The essay uses two true stories as supporting materials, which are both very appropriate and powerful.

There is a theory about the structure of classical Chinese poetry, which goes "beginning, developing, turning, and closing." A persuasive essay is also often composed of these four parts. The four paragraphs of this piece play precisely these four functions. The first paragraph is the beginning, which proposes the argument. The second paragraph is the development, which continues to explain the affirmative point. The third paragraph is the turning, which criticizes the opposing point. The fourth paragraph is the closing, drawing a conclusion. Because of its well-organized structure and clearly defined progression, it reads with good momentum and is quite convincing.

词汇三

1	对照	對照	duìzhào	to contrast, compare
2	有力		yǒulì	strong, powerful
3	作法		zuòfǎ	technique of writing, art of composition
4	起		qǐ	to start, begin, initiate
5	承		chéng	to continue, carry on
6	转	轉	zhuǎn	to turn, shift
7	合		hé	to close, conclude
8	说（法）	說（法）	shuōfa	way of saying something, statement, theory
9	部分		bùfen	part, section, portion
10	构成	構成	gòuchéng	to constitute, form, compose
11	功能		gōngnéng	function
12	批驳	批駁	pībó	to criticize, refute
13	充沛		chōngpèi	plentiful, abundant
14	令人		lìngrén	使人, make someone
15	信服		xìnfú	to be convinced
16	令人信服		lìngrén xìnfú	convincing

7.4 Rhetoric 修辞

Rhetorical question 反问

写作时，有时为了引起读者注意，故意先提出问题。问句常常能造成强烈的效果，还能启发读者思考，也可以加强作者想表达的思想。例如："中文难吗？其实不难。"本课范文的第一句 和最后一句也都是问句。

　　反问句实际上是强调某种肯定或否定的答案,也就是明知故问。这类句式常用 "难道," "怎么" 等反问词。例如："难道中文有这么难么？"—说话者在强调中文不难。课文中的"自知之明不正是自信与自负的分界线吗？" 就是反问句。

In writing, sometimes in order to catch the readers' attention, one should purposely raise a question first. In addition to making a dramatic effect, questions can often inspire readers to think, and it can also strengthen the expression of the author's ideas. For example, "Is Chinese difficult? Indeed, it is not." An additional example is that both the first and last sentence of the main text of this lesson are questions.

Rhetorical questions actually function to emphasize certain affirmative or negative answers, which is also to purposely ask a question with a clear answer. In these sentences, certain rhetorical words such as *nandao* (is it possible) and *zenme* (how) are often used. For example, "Is it possible that Chinese is so difficult?" – here, the speaker is emphasizing that Chinese is not difficult. The sentence in the text, "Isn't self-awareness the boundary of confidence and conceit?" is also a rhetorical question.

词汇四

1	引起		yǐnqǐ	to cause, arouse, generate
2	故意		gùyì	intentionally, on purpose,
3	读者	讀者	dúzhě	reader
4	加强	加強	jiāqiáng	to enhance, strengthen
5	例如		lìrú	for example
6	否定		fǒudìng	negative, denial
7	答案		dá'àn	answer
8	明（明）		míng(míng)	obviously, undoubtedly
9	故		gù	故意，intentionally
10	明知故问	明知故問	míngzhī gùwèn	to ask while knowing the answer
11	类	類	lèi	kind, type
12	句式		jùshì	syntactical structure

7.5 Practical writing 应用文

Reader response 读后感

我们读了一本书、一篇文章，把得到的感受和启示写成文章，就是读后感。看了一个电影、戏剧后所写的感想，也可以归入读后感中。

　　要写好读后感，要在 "读" 和 "感" 两个字上下功夫。首先是读，要深刻理解作品内容及其主旨。其次是感，写出自己独特、真实的感想。写读后感不是写书评，不需要作全面的评论和介绍，只要写出你感受最深的一点或几点。写作时常常夹叙夹议，也可适当结合抒情。

After reading a book or an article, we write about what we feel and how we have been inspired, and this is the reader response. Writing about thoughts after watching a movie or a play can also be included in reader response.

In order to write a reader response well, one should put effort into both reading the original work and writing about his or her thoughts. First is reading – one needs to deeply understand the content and purpose of the work. Second is thought – to write one's own unique and true views. A reader response is not a book review; one does not need to make a comprehensive commentary and introduction, but only needs to write one or more opinions which he or she feels most strongly about. When writing, one often intersperses comments within narration and may also express feelings whenever necessary and appropriate.

词汇五

1	感受		gǎnshòu	feeling, impression, reflection
2	启示	啟示	qǐshì	enlightenment, inspiration
3	归入	歸入	guīrù	to be included in
4	原作		yuánzuò	original work
5	其		qí	his, her, its, their
6	主旨		zhǔzhǐ	purport, gist
7	其次		qícì	next, secondly
8	独特	獨特	dútè	unique, distinctive
9	书评	書評	shūpíng	book review
10	评论	評論	pínglùn	commentary, review, critique
11	夹	夾	jiā	to mix, mingle, intersperse
12	夹叙夹议	夾敘夾議	jiāxù jiāyì	narration interspersed with comments

7.6 Vocabulary training 词汇训练

一、填宾语 Fill in the blanks with appropriate objects to form verb-object phrases.

1 支持 ＿＿＿＿
2 显示 ＿＿＿＿
3 激发 ＿＿＿＿
4 培养 ＿＿＿＿
5 启发 ＿＿＿＿
6 剖析 ＿＿＿＿
7 承认 ＿＿＿＿
8 战胜 ＿＿＿＿
9 比较 ＿＿＿＿
10 导致 ＿＿＿＿
11 肯定 ＿＿＿＿
12 充满 ＿＿＿＿
13 辨别 ＿＿＿＿
14 了解 ＿＿＿＿
15 参加 ＿＿＿＿
16 指挥 ＿＿＿＿
17 发现 ＿＿＿＿
18 祝贺 ＿＿＿＿

19 设计 ____
20 检验 ____
21 摘取 ____
22 征服 ____
23 缺乏 ____
24 区分 ____
25 批驳 ____
26 引起 ____
27 提出 ____
28 加强 ____
29 强调 ____
30 理解 ____

二、选词填空 Fill in the blanks with the words provided.

2 论点要明确，论据要充分，论证要 ____ 。

   a. 严密   c. 严厉
   b. 严格   d. 严重

3 苦可以激发 ____ 心。

   a. 自尊   c. 进取
   b. 同情   d. 责任

4 苦可以培养 ____ 的意志。

   a. 坚决   c. 坚硬
   b. 坚强   d. 坚固

5 初看起来，自信的人与自负的人都对自我高度肯定，对自己的水平与能力 ____ 信心。

   a. 充分   c. 充实
   b. 充足   d. 充满

6 两者的差别往往是细微的，但实际上也是巨大的，并且是可以 ____ 的。

   a. 分别   c. 差别
   b. 辨别   d. 离别

7 一个人的自信是基于对自己的能力的充分而正确的 ____ 。

   a. 理解   c. 讲解
   b. 了解   d. 见解

8 他按照评委会给的乐谱指挥演奏，敏锐地发现了不 ____ 的声音。

   a. 和谐   c. 和平
   b. 和睦   d. 和好

9 话音刚落，评委们立即站起来， ____ 鼓掌，祝贺他大赛夺魁。

   a. 热情   c. 热烈
   b. 热闹   d. 热爱

10 原来，这是评委们 ＿＿＿ 设计的 "圈套," 以此来检验指挥家的能力。

    a. 精彩　　c. 精妙
    b. 精心　　d. 精确

11 所以说，自信是一个人事业成功的 ＿＿＿ 。

    a. 保证　　c. 见证
    b. 论证　　d. 认证

12 法兰西第一帝国的 ＿＿＿ 者拿破仑是个军事天才。

    a. 建造　　c. 修造
    b. 制造　　d. 缔造

13 拿破仑一度征服大半个 ＿＿＿ 。

    a. 亚洲　　c. 美洲
    b. 非洲　　d. 欧洲

14 滑铁卢惨败后，拿破仑被流放到 ＿＿＿ 的一个岛上。

    a. 太平洋　c. 印度洋
    b. 大西洋　d. 北冰洋

15 自信的人却充满 ＿＿＿ 又谦虚谨慎，一步一个脚印地往前走。

    a. 能力　　c. 活力
    b. 动力　　d. 电力

16 问句除了能引起注意外，还能启发读者 ＿＿＿ 。

    a. 思想　　c. 思念
    b. 思考　　d. 思虑

三、改错 Correct the errors.

1 演绎法，即用几个平行的分论点来支持中心论点，以显示思维的全面性。
2 归纳法，即将事理分解成正反两个方面，以显示思维的鲜明性。
3 自信与自负的差别往往是巨大的，并且是可以辨别的。
4 小泽征尔年轻时参加一次国际钢琴大赛。
5 小泽征尔因充满自信而摘取了世界指挥家大赛的皇冠。
6 自负的人，是对自己取得的成绩和聪明程度缺乏自信。
7 法兰西第二帝国的缔造者拿破仑是个军事天才。
8 有一次拿破仑在过喜马拉雅山时说 "我比喜马拉雅山还要高！"
9 文中用了两个真实的故事作为论点，非常贴切、有力。
10 反问句实际上是强调某种肯定或否定的答案,也就是自问自答。

7.7 Phrase training 语句训练

一、用句型造句 Make sentences using the following sentence patterns.

1 往往 ...... 但实际上 ...... 并且

    【课文例句】两者的差别往往是细微的，但实际上也是巨大的，并且是可以辨别的。

【生活例句】白春梅往往说她中文学得不好，但实际上她讲话很流利，并且字也写得很好。

Bai Chunmei often says that she does not study Chinese very well, but actually she speaks fluently and also writes characters very well.

2   ......所以说

【课文例句】小泽征尔因充满自信而摘取了世界指挥家大赛的桂冠。所以说，自信是一个人事业成功的保证。
【生活例句】赵经理工作很努力，事业上也很有成就，可是这么年轻就去世了，所以说，健康是最重要的，是事业的保证。

Manager Zhao worked very hard and had also achieved much in his career, but he passed away at such a young age. Therefore, health is most important and is the foundation of a career.

3   的确......但......最后

【课文例句】的确，他一度征服大半个欧洲，但他的自负使他无限制的扩张，最后在滑铁卢惨败，被流放到大西洋的一个岛上。
【生活例句】他小学的学习成绩的确很好，但中学时整天玩电脑游戏，最后连大学都没考上，太可惜了。

His grades in elementary school were indeed very good, but he played computer games all day in middle school and high school, so, in the end, he could not even get into college. How pitiful!

4   往往......又

【课文例句】自负的人往往狂妄自大、目空一切，说的比做的多，又只想听好话。
【生活例句】中文学得好的人往往比较聪明，又努力，所以别的课程也会学得好的。

Those who study Chinese well are often smart and diligent, therefore they can also study other courses well.

5   除了能......还能......也可以

【课文例句】设问除了能引起注意外，还能启发读者思考，也可以加强作者想表达的思想。
【生活例句】他游泳游得很好，除了能游自由泳，还能游蛙泳，也可以游蝶泳。

He is a good swimmer. In addition to freestyle, he can also do the breaststroke, as well as the butterfly stroke.

6   实际上是......也就是

【课文例句】反问句实际上是强调某种肯定或否定的答案、也就是明知故问。
【生活例句】我家的邻居王老先生喜欢在园子里种花、种蔬菜，实际上是活动腿脚，也就是锻炼身体。

Our neighbor, the old Mr. Wang, likes to grow flowers and vegetables. Actually, he wants to keep active, which is indeed a good exercise.

7 要......（就）要

【课文例句】要写好读后感，要在 "读" 和 "感" 两个字上下功夫。
【生活例句】要身体健康，就要在饮食和锻炼上多下功夫。

If you want to keep healthy, you should pay more attention to food and exercise.

8 首先......其次

【课文例句】首先是读，要读懂原作，深刻理解作品内容及其主旨。其次是感，写出自己独特、真实的感想。
【生活例句】要唱好一首歌，首先是要唱得自然，其次是要唱出这首歌的感情。

If you want to sing a song well, first you need to sing naturally, and then you need to express the mood of the song.

9 不是......不需要......只要

【课文例句】写读后感不是写书评，不需要作全面的评论和介绍，只要写出你感受最深的一点或几点。
【生活例句】我学唱歌不是想成为一个歌唱家，不需要进行太正规的声乐训练，只要自己唱得开心就行。

I don't practice singing to be a professional singer, so I do not need very formal vocal training. It's fine as long as singing makes me happy.

二、回答问题Answer the questions.

1 议论文有哪三个要素？
2 什么是归纳法？
3 什么是演绎法？
4 什么是比较法？
5 自信的人与自负的人有什么相同的地方？
6 小泽征尔是怎样摘取了世界指挥家大赛的桂冠的？
7 自信与自负的分界线是什么？
8 自负的实质是什么？
9 怎样区分自信与自负？
10 本课课文是一篇用什么法子写的议论文？
11 请说明本课课文 "起承转合" 的结构。
12 什么叫设问句？
13 设问句有什么作用？
14 反问句常用哪些反问词？
15 什么是读后感？什么是观后感？
16 怎样才能写好读后感？
17 读后感和书评有什么区别？

三、翻译设问诗句 Translate these poetic lines with questions.
The following three couplets are quoted from famous ancient poems. All of them begin with a question. Please translate these poetic lines into modern Chinese.

1 明月几时有？把酒问青天。（苏轼《水调歌头》）
2 问君能有几多愁？恰似一江春水向东流。（李煜《虞美人》）
3 日暮乡关何处是？烟波江上使人愁。（崔颢《黄鹤楼》）

7.8 Composition training 作文训练

一、仿写作文 *Imitative composition*

写一篇题为《事业和健康》的论说文，要符合以下三个要求：1. 你的文章应讨论健康和事业的关系；2. 要用上论证三法之一：归纳法、演绎法或比较法；3. 用例子支持你的论点。

Write a persuasive essay titled "Health and Career," following three requirements: 1. Your essay should discuss the relationship between health and career. 2. Use one of the three ways of argumentation: induction, deduction, or comparison. 3. Use examples to support your arguments.

二、情景作文 *Situational composition*

假设你参加了一个辩论队。辩论的题目是"自信与自负."选边站队并写下你的辩论稿。

Suppose you are on a debate team and the debate topic is "Confidence and Conceit." Choose one side and write your debate points.

三、串联作文 *Chain story composition*

这个练习是全班同学作为课外作业的集体创作。根据姓名的英文字母的排列，每人依次写一句。论文会放在"黑板"或其他类似的课堂教学管理系统的讨论板上。论文的开端提供在下面。尽量使文章易懂、逻辑性强和生动有趣。尽可能多用反问句。你一看到你前面的同学写好了，就应着手写作。一圈下来，轮到的任何人只要觉得故事应该到此为止，就可以结束故事。此后，班上要举行一次讨论。

This will be a collective story created by the whole class as homework. According to the alphabetical order of the class list, each writer is succeeded by the next student. The article will be posted on the discussion board on Blackboard©. The beginning of the article is provided below. Try to make the article understandable, logical, and interesting. Use rhetorical questions to the best of your ability. You should begin to write your sentence as soon as you see the preceding one completed. After the first round, anybody during his or her turn can conclude the story if he or she thinks it's right place to do so. A class discussion of the story will follow.

题目：《学历与能力》

在每份申请工作的简历上，首先映入眼帘的往往是申请者的学历。学历当然是衡量一个人的工作能力的重要标志，但是学历和能力的关系到底是怎样的呢？……

四、进阶作文 *Sequential composition*

以《论电脑游戏》为题目，写三篇短文。

Write three short pieces in sequence with the title of "On Computer Games."

1　写一个100字左右的段落，说明你对电脑游戏的利弊的看法。

　　Write a paragraph of about 100 characters, stating your view of the pros and cons of computer games.

2　写两个100字左右的段落，提出两个分论点以及支持的论据。

　　Write a short piece with two 100-character paragraphs, proposing two sub-arguments as well as providing supporting evidence.

3　结合上述三个段落的内容，用论证三法中之一法，写一篇500字左右的小论文。

　　Combine the contents of the two aforementioned pieces, and write a persuasive essay of about 500 characters, using one of the three methods of argumentation.

五、应用文写作 *Practical composition*

写一篇读后感。

Write a reader response.

Appendices 附录

English translations of the model texts 范文英译

Lesson one

An amusing account of examination preparations

Tomorrow is our business law class' final exam. This is the course I fear the most, as I have to mechanically memorize many articles of law. Oh well, I will be living in the library tonight, and preparing for the exam throughout the entire night.

At 11 p.m., I vigorously walked to the library, found a quiet corner, and sat down on a sofa. I pulled out two cans of "Red Bull" from my backpack and stood them on the low table before me so that they were like two soldiers with strong fighting spirits, safeguarding my time. Ancient people worked through the night, having to "tie their hair to the house beam and poke their thighs with an awl," but modern students need not suffer this sort of cruelty.

Upon opening the brick-like textbook, my iPhone in my pocket began to vibrate. At a glance, I saw my good friend Laura had sent me a text message: "Where are you?" I thought, two people reviewing together could be good, as we can go back and forth asking and answering questions and helping each other to remember the content.

As soon as Laura sat down, she complained to me about the Chinese test from this afternoon. When answering the question about "Your Aspiration," she originally wanted to write *dashi* (ambassador), but she wasn't careful and wrote the *shi* character as *bian*. As soon as I heard this, I could not control my laughter. We ridiculed each other's mistakes on the Chinese exam, and in no time it was already midnight.

We immediately started asking and answering questions. Laura had just asked me: "Where was the first bankruptcy law enacted?" when suddenly we heard a person call: "Here!" Shortly, two of my other good friends, Linda and Lisa, unexpectedly approached. As soon as they both sat down, they said that after the exam was over we certainly should go someplace that would be fun. So, the four of us began discussing travel plans. In the end, we decided to go on a Florida cruise. By then it was already 2 a.m., and my stomach began to protest. Linda said: "If your stomach is empty, how can you study? We should go to the Bubble Tea shop and get a midnight snack!"

We returned after eating our midnight snack, and the hour hand pointed to 3 a.m. Business law proved to be extremely boring. We had just asked and answered a few questions when everyone's drooping eyelids fought to stay open. Looking at the two empty Red Bull cans lying about the table, Lisa said: "Now, even if you drink another ten Red Bulls it will be of no use. Now your stomach is full and your head is empty. It's better to take a short nap, and when you wake up your head will be clear and we can review again." Her words were justified, and so everyone lay down on the sofa to rest.

I only heard Laura shouting: "This isn't good! It's 7:30!" Everyone quickly jumped up, stuffed their books into their backpacks, tossed the Red Bull cans into the trash bin, and rushed to the classroom. Our business law exam starts at 8 a.m.!

Lesson two

A tune in the rain

In Chinese class, our teacher said that we would have to perform a skit tomorrow, and he assigned me and Mark to prepare it together. When class ended, we hastily made plans to meet tonight at 8 p.m. to practice, even without time to talk about the place

Who knew, after eating dinner and returning to my dorm, a violent wind gusted outside my window and dark clouds rolled in. As lightning flashed and thunder crashed, giant raindrops fell from the sky, and lashed against the window like a whip.

I called Mark, hoping to ask him where we should meet, but my cellphone lost signal. What horrible weather! It would soon be 7:45 p.m., and my roommate, Tom, pointed to the window saying, "Look, the roads outside have turned into the Yellow River and the Yangtze River, must you really go out? Mark is definitely staying inside and watching TV." I said, "Then I will go to his dorm. We must practice. How else will we perform the skit tomorrow?" Upon saying this, I gathered up my courage, grabbed an umbrella, and charged out the door.

Without taking many steps, a large gust of wind hit me and blew my umbrella inside out. With great difficulty I was able to turn the umbrella back, but I had become soaked to the bone like a chicken drenched in water. In the movie, "Singin' in the Rain," the actor takes an umbrella and dances while singing, and this has become a beloved classic passed down through generations. If he were in this heavy downpour, he'd be unable to dance.

My face was greeted by a big gust of wind. It was all I could do to put the umbrella in front of me, lower my head and walk forward. Unexpectedly, I stepped into a puddle, my stance became unsteady, and I fell down. I climbed back up, and already my face was stained with mud and I couldn't see clearly. At this time my face must have looked like a Beijing opera star's painted face.

When I reached Mark's dorm, water flowed continuously off my body and immediately accumulated in a puddle at my feet. I knocked on the door and thought, "In any event, we will practice well."

In a moment, Mark's roommate opened the door. Upon glancing at me, his face was filled with doubt. "Why did you come? Mark went to your dorm!"

Lesson three

Mother's smiles

Ever since I can remember, my mother always has had a smile on her face. When she smiles, the two corners of her mouth slightly curl upward, and her two big eyes reveal a faint smile within. Upon seeing my mother's smile, I feel happy, content, and safe.

During elementary school, when I returned home after the school day ended I was greeted by my mother's smile. When I got off the school bus, my mother was next to the driveway waiting for me. She held my hand, looked at me with her smile, and it seemed as if she asked in that moment, "Did today go well?"

During middle and high school, I often participated in piano competitions and recitals. From the time I stepped out on stage, my heart leapt into my throat, and I took a glimpse of the auditorium below out of the corners of my eyes. My mother smiled and nodded in my direction, seemingly saying, "Don't worry. You'll play great."

During college, I video called my mother every day. I would tell her about whatever happened during that day, such as how the day's test went, if I made another new friend, etc. Upon seeing my mother's smile attentively listening to me, I felt that the day went well.

There were also times when my mother didn't smile. Once when I was young, I had an exceptionally high fever. My mother sat by my bedside throughout the whole night without closing her eyes. One moment she would take my temperature, and the next give me water to drink, all the while both of her eyes were bright red. On the morning of the second day, my fever went away, and only when my mother saw the thermometer did a slight smile appear in her rosy eyes.

Another time when she didn't smile was during my senior year of high school. My boyfriend had just gotten his driver's license, and he was very excited so he wanted to take me out for a joyride. At noon we went to McDonald's for lunch and got into the car again to shop at Walmart. As a result, I didn't attend any of my afternoon classes. Only when my teacher called my home did my mother find out what I did. When I came home that day, the smile disappeared from my mother's face.

My mother's smile is a mild spring breeze, is a clear spring in the summer, is a bright star in a long night, and is a harbor in a storm. I know that my mother's smile will always accompany me as I continue on my prolonged life path.

Lesson four

Impressions of Niagara Falls

This past summer, my whole family and I went to see Niagara Falls. We drove through Buffalo, a city on the American-Canadian border, and not long after we gazed upon the world-famous waterfalls. From afar they looked like a white veil, hanging among blue mountains and green waters. No wonder one of the falls is called the "Bridal Veil Falls."

Nearing the falls, we first took the "Maiden of the Mist" cruise to enjoy the view of the falls. With the falls pouring down right in front of our faces, I couldn't help but think of Li Bai's poem of a waterfall that we learned in Chinese class: "The water flying down 3,000 feet, I suspected it was the Milky Way falling from the highest of Heavens." At this time, I could only see the torrents of the waterfall and spray splashing up and diffusing into mist. I could only hear the roaring water and the screaming and cheering passengers. When the boat steered towards the falls, I could only think that just this waterfall existed between Heaven and Earth, and I had already transformed into a single drop of water within it.

After disembarking, we went to visit the Canadian "Journey Behind the Falls." We rode an elevator down dozens of meters deep underground, went along a tunnel and came upon a protruding platform, when suddenly the falls appeared right by my side! "Hey," I thought, "isn't this just like the Monkey King's Water Curtain Cave in 'Journey to the West'?" With the thunderstorm right in our faces, it seemed that using the idioms "a ladle of water pouring down" and "a basin of water pouring down" to describe it would be too light. This was simply a giant overturning the Great Lakes, letting all the water pour out and down.

Niagara Falls at night is yet another scene. Illuminated by the surrounding colorful spot-lights, it appears more colorful than during the day. The falls are like hundreds of millions of pearls transforming colors as the lights hits them. From white it turns to pink, from pink it turns to sky-blue, from sky-blue it turns to grass-green. It's very colorful and ever changing, and the magnificent waterfalls are turned into a magical wonderland.

Lesson five

Autumn colors on campus

Our campus is beautiful throughout all four seasons, but the most beautiful is autumn.

In September and October, the trees on the surrounding hills are dyed golden and red. Gazing upon them from a distance, they seem to be covered in gorgeous velvet set against a blue sky laden with white clouds, leaving one to admire the grandiose creativity of nature.

On campus, the grass is still green, but spotted with golden leaves. A gust of wind blows, and another burst of leaves float down, like a swarm of golden butterflies fluttering through the air. The ground before the red brick school building is covered with a layer of leaves, which looks like an oil painting and is reminiscent of the alluring scene of an old European university.

Flowerbeds, both large and small, add various new colors. Look, there is an area full of chrysanthemums. There is red and pink, but of course there is mostly golden yellow. The Chinese use the phrase, "The autumn chrysanthemum braves the frost," to praise the flower's nature of not fearing the cold.

Aside from the vegetation, life on campus during autumn is just as colorful. Students emerge from the summer slumber, adjust, and with renewed energy return to school, so campus is filled with vigor. On the campus' main pathway, there are students carrying back-packs and rushing around. On the big lawn under the Bell Tower, there is a class in session. Students sitting on the grass in a circle are bathed in the golden autumn sun.

If you wanted to choose a color for the fall campus, I would choose gold. Gold makes people think of a field full of waves of billowing wheat, which is of the harvest season. Gold makes people think of a royal crown, which is a symbol of loyalty. But at the moment, gold is the fallen leaves covering the roads, it is the smiling face of the blossoming chrysan-themum, and it is the soft and pleasant sunshine. Gold makes people feel the warmth and richness of life.

Lesson six

Musical charm

This winter break, I attended a concert at the National Theater in Beijing. The program's grand finale is the violin concerto "The Butterfly Lovers." We had just learned about this story in our Chinese class last semester, where the teacher had introduced this famous musical piece to us. Now we have the opportunity to enjoy the performance of the Chinese National Symphony Orchestra within this resplendent and magnificent concert hall. I feel so excited that I may transform into a butterfly.

When the program started, the violin played the theme of the piece. Altogether there were only four movements, which were very graceful and smooth, causing one to feel Liang Shanbo and Zhu Yingtai's yearning for a happy life and true love. This portion of music is very simple and rich in poetic sentiment, and it's as if one could see the lovers strolling by the river, on the small bridge beneath the willow tree gazing at the fish and studying beside the window bathed in the glow of the sunset. This type of inseparable and deep love struck my heartstrings. At the same time, these movements also contain intricacy, revealing some sadness and foreshadowing the approaching misfortune.

The cello's natural and resonant tone subsequently joined, and carried out an exchange with the violin solo, describing a scene of mutual love and affinity felt by Liang and Zhu. The music would separate and join interchangeably, at times being very touching and distressed. Suddenly, the music took a turn for the worse, using a variety of instruments and measures to convey the disapproval of Zhu Yingtai's father, Yingtai's resistance to an arranged marriage, Shanbo's death by illness, and finally Yingtai's suicide. The violin projected the sound of being torn by grief and heartbreak, depicting the scene where Zhu Yingtai is crying before Liang Shanbo's grave, resulting in an atmosphere of intense tragedy.

The final part of the song is called "Transformation into Butterflies," where the two butterfly lovers fly out of the grave and transform into a pair of butterflies, flying freely amongst the flowers. This time the theme of love in the piece possessed a lighthearted, hazy, and sublime character, symbolizing a wonderful dream world, but also expressing feelings of infinite nostalgia and reverence. The repeated performance of the theme of love makes this feeling continue to be sublimated.

Lesson seven

Confidence and conceit

What is the difference between confidence and conceit? There is literally only one different character between the two words. At first glance, confident people and conceited people are both very sure of themselves and are filled with confidence in their own ability. The difference between the two is often very subtle but is actually also very great and discernable.

A person's confidence is based on the fullest, yet most proper, understanding of one's ability. The famous symphony conductor, Seiji Ozawa, once in his youth participated in a big conductor competition. He conducted according to the musical score that was provided by the judges, and keenly discerned the inharmonious tones and thought the music had a problem. However, a group of authoritative judges insisted that the score was absolutely perfect, and that he was wrong. Facing a large group of musical masters, he firmly said, "No! Certainly the music is wrong!" As his voice faded, the judges immediately stood, warmly applauded, and congratulated him on winning first place. As it turns out, the judges had set up an elaborate trap, in order to test the ability of the conductor. Because young Seiji Ozawa was fully confident, he obtained the honor as champion of the world conductor's competition. So it is said that confidence guarantees a person's success.

Conceited people are over-confident in their achievements and their level of intellect. The founder of the first French empire, Napoleon Bonaparte, was a military genius. Once when he was in the Alps, he said, "I am higher than the Alps!" Indeed, he had at a time conquered most of Europe, however his conceit caused him to excessively expand, and finally he suffered a disastrous defeat at Waterloo and was exiled to an island in the Atlantic Ocean. To think of oneself too highly and look down upon one's rivals more often than not leads to that conceited person's failure.

There is a saying that goes, "It's important to know one's self." Is knowledge of oneself not the boundary between being confident and being conceited? The essence of conceit is ignorance and is a lack of correct assessment of the ability of oneself and others. Then, how can one distinguish between confidence and conceit? Conceited people are often wildly arrogant and supercilious. They say more than they do, and they only want to hear compliments. Confident people are filled with vigor, and are modest and prudent, moving forward step by step. Which kind of person do you want to be?

Vocabulary index 词汇索引

创造	創造	chuàngzào	to create, produce	7.1
创造力	創造力	chuàngzàolì	creativity	5.2
淳朴	淳樸	chúnpǔ	simple and plain	6.2
辞藻	辭藻	cízǎo	expressions in literary writings	5.5
此		cǐ	这, 这个 this	1.2
刺		cì	to stab, prick	1.2
匆匆		cōngcōng	hastily, in a hurry	2.2
从...起	從...起	cóng ... qǐ	from ... on	3.2
从...上讲	從...上講	cóng ... shàng jiǎng	to speak in the perspective of to exist	6.1
存在		cúnzài		4.2
寸		cùn	A unit of length (1/30 meter)	6.2

D

搭乘		dāchéng	to ride	4.2
答案		dá'àn	answer	7.4
打盹儿	打盹兒	dǎdǔnr	to doze off, take a nap	1.2
打架		dǎjià	to fight	1.2
大师	大師	dàshī	master	7.2
大西洋		Dàxīyáng	Atlantic Ocean	7.2
大展宏图	大展宏圖	dàzhǎn hóngtú	to realize one's ambition	2.5
呆		dāi	to stay	2.2
诞（生）	誕（生）	dàn(shēng)	birth	6.4
党	黨	dǎng	party	1.2
当做	當做	dàngzuò	to treat as, regard as	1.4
岛	島	dǎo	island	7.2
导致	導致	dǎozhì	to cause, result in	7.1
道		dào	a flash of	2.2
倒叙	倒敘	dàoxù	flashback	1.1
帝国	帝國	dìguó	empire	7.2
递进	遞進	dìjìn	to progressively move forward	2.3
地区		dìqū	area, region	4.1
缔造者	締造者	dìzào zhě	founder	7.2
点击	點擊	diǎnjī	to click (a computer mouse button)	1.5
点评	點評	diǎnpíng	critique, commentary	1.3
点燃	點燃	diǎnrán	to light, kindle, ignite	6.4
点题	點題	diǎntí	to refer back to the title, bring out the theme	5.2
典型		diǎnxíng	typical, representative	4.4
点缀	點綴	diǎnzhuì	to embellish, intersperse	5.2
电梯	電梯	diàntī	elevator	4.2
掉		diào	to drop, fall	4.4
东倒西歪	東倒西歪	dōngdǎo xīwāi	to waver east and west, fall over like ninepins	1.2
动手	動手	dòngshǒu	to get to work, to do	4.5
动作	動作	dòngzuò	movement, action	3.1
冻死	凍死	dòngsǐ	to freeze to death	6.4
兜风	兜風	dōufēng	to go for a (joy) ride	3.2
豆		dòu	bean	2.2
斗志昂扬	鬥志昂揚	dòuzhì ángyáng	to have a strong fighting spirit, have high morale	1.2
独特	獨特	dútè	unique, distinctive	7.5
读者	讀者	dúzhě	reader	7.4
短信		duǎnxìn	short message	1.2
断	斷	duàn	to break	2.4
断肠	斷腸	duàncháng	heartbroken	5.1

段落		duànluò	paragraph	1.5
对答	對答	duìdá	to answer, respond	6.2
对方	對方	duìfāng	other side, opposite side	5.5
对 . . . 来说	對 . . . 來說	duì . . . láishuō	to, regarding	1.5
对手	對手	duìshǒu	opponent, rival	7.2
对照	對照	duìzhào	to contrast, compare	7.3
多姿多彩		duōzī duōcǎi	charming and colorful	4.2
夺	奪	duó	to take by force, seize, wrest	7.2
夺魁	奪魁	duókuí	to come first, win first prize, win the championship	7.2

E

扼要		èyào	concise, to the point, brief, and precise	1.5

F

发	發	fā	to send, deliver	1.2
发挥	發揮	fāhuī	to bring into play, give free rein to	5.3
发烧	發燒	fāshāo	to have a fever or temperature	3.2
发生	發生	fāshēng	to occur, take place	1.1
发送	發送	fāsòng	to send, transmit	1.5
法		fǎ	法律, law	1.2
法宝	法寶	fǎbǎo	talisman, trump	1.3
法兰西	法蘭西	Fǎlánxī	France	7.2
法子		fǎzi	way, method	1.1
翻		fān	to turn (over, up, inside out, etc.)	1.4
翻滚	翻滾	fāngǔn	to roll, tumble	2.2
翻飞	翻飛	fānfēi	to fly up and down	5.2
翻转	翻轉	fānzhuǎn	to overturn	4.2
反映		fǎnyìng	to reflect	1.5
范文	範文	fànwén	model essay	1.2
仿佛		fǎngfú	as if	6.2
放大		fàngdà	to enlarge, magnify	4.4
飞溅	飛濺	fēijiàn	to splash, spatter	4.2
分		fēn	subordinate	7.1
分解		fēnjiě	to separate into parts, break up	7.1
分界线	分界線	fēnjièxiàn	line of demarcation, boundary	7.2
坟	墳	fén	grave, tomb	6.2
坟墓	墳墓	fénmù	grave, tomb	6.2
粉		fěn	pink	3.4
粉红	粉紅	fěnhóng	pink	4.2
风景线	風景線	fēngjǐngxiàn	view, scenery line	5.3
丰满	豐滿	fēngmǎn	full, plentiful	2.3
丰收	豐收	fēngshōu	bumper harvest	5.2
逢		féng	to meet, encounter	2.5
逢年过节	逢年過節	féngnián guòjié	on New Year's Day or other festivals	2.5
否定		fǒudìng	negative, denial	7.4
福		fú	blessing, good fortune	2.5
幅		fú	a measure word for cloth, painting, etc.	4.2
拂		fú	to stroke, caress	6.2
佛罗里达	佛羅裏達	Fúluólǐdá	Florida	1.2
腹		fù	abdomen, belly	1.2
附件		fùjiàn	attachment	4.5
富有		fùyǒu	rich in, full of	6.2
富于		fùyú	to be rich in, be full of	1.1
赋予	賦予	fùyǔ	to endow, give	6.4
赴约	赴約	fùyuē	to go to an appointment	2.2

G

盖	蓋	gài	to build, construct	4.4
概述		gàishù	outline, summary	2.1
肝		gān	liver	6.2
肝肠寸断	肝腸寸斷	gāncháng cùnduàn	deeply grieved, heartbroken	6.2
感觉	感覺	gǎnjué	feeling, sense perception	5.1
感情		gǎnqíng	emotion, feeling, affection	2.1
感受		gǎnshòu	feeling, impression, reflection	7.5
感叹	感歎	gǎntàn	to sign with feeling, exclaim	6.1
感叹词	感歎詞	gǎntàncí	interjection, exclamation	6.1
港湾	港灣	gǎngwān	harbor	3.2
高潮		gāocháo	climax	3.3
高度		gāodù	highly	7.2
高原		gāoyuán	plateau	4.1
格式		géshì	format, layout	1.5
格外		géwài	especially, particularly	6.4
根据	根據	gēnjù	on the basis of, according to	1.4
功能		gōngnéng	function	7.3
宫阙		gōngquè	imperial palace	5.4
钩	鈎	gōu	hook, *measure word for the crescent moon*	5.4
构成	構成	gòuchéng	to constitute, form, compose	7.3
孤陋寡闻	孤陋寡聞	gūlòu guǎwén	ignorant and ill-informed	7.1
股		gǔ	大腿, thigh	1.2
鼓		gǔ	drum, to strike or play a music instrument	7.2
鼓起勇气	鼓起勇氣	gǔqǐ yǒngqì	to pluck up one's courage	2.2
鼓掌		gǔzhǎng	to applaud	7.2
故		gù	故意	7.4
故意		gùyì	intentionally, on purpose,	7.4
冠		guān	帽子 hat	7.2
关爱	關愛	guān'ài	love and care	3.3
观察	觀察	guānchá	to observe, watch	4.1
关键	關鍵	guānjiàn	key, crux	3.1
观赏	觀賞	guānshǎng	观看欣赏 view, admire	4.2
关系	關系	guānxì	relation, connection	5.4
观众席	觀衆席	guānzhòngxí	auditorium (of a theater), grandstand (of a stadium)	3.2
罐		guàn	jar, can	1.2
光辉	光輝	guānghuī	brilliant, shining	2.5
光明磊落		guāngmíng lěiluò	frank and forthright	5.4
归纳	歸納	guīnà	induction	7.1
归入	歸入	guīrù	to be included in	7.5
规则	規則	guīzé	rule, regulation	1.5
鬼		guǐ	terrible, nasty (weather, place, etc.)	2.2
贵	貴	guì	valuable, precious, important	7.1
桂		guì	cassia, laurel	7.2
桂冠		guìguān	laurel	7.2
国家大剧院	國家大劇院	Guójiā dà jùyuàn	National Center for the Performing Arts	6.2
过分	過分	guòfèn	excessive, extreme	7.2

H

海报	海報	hǎibào	poster	4.5
寒冷		hánlěng	chilly, frigid	5.2
寒暄语	寒暄語	hánxuānyǔ	pleasantries	1.5
含蓄		hánxù	implicit	6.1

行		háng	line, row	1.5
豪华	豪華	háohuá	luxurious	1.2
豪华游轮	豪華遊輪	háohuá yóulún	cruise	1.2
豪言壮语	豪言壯語	háoyán zhuàngyǔ	heroic words	5.5
好不容易		hǎobùróngyì	with great difficulty	2.2
号	號	hào	mark, sign	1.5
何		hé	what	5.4
何必		hébì	used in rhetorical questions to indicate that there is no need to do something	2.2
合		hé	to close, conclude	7.3
和谐	和諧	héxié	harmonious	7.2
和煦		héxù	genial, pleasantly warm	3.2
贺词	賀詞	hècí	speech of congratulation	2.5
贺卡	賀卡	hèkǎ	greeting card	2.5
黑莓		Hēiméi	BlackBerry	1.2
横	橫	héng	horizontal, transverse	1.2
轰鸣	轟鳴	hōngmíng	to roar, thunder	4.2
宏		hóng	great, grand, magnificent	2.5
红牛	紅牛	Hóngniú	Red Bull (an energy drink)	1.2
蝴蝶		húdié	butterfly	5.2
胡琴		húqín	a two-stringed, bowed instrument	6.2
花脸	花臉	huāliǎn	painted face (in Beijing opera)	2.2
花坛	花壇	huātán	flower bed, flower terrace	5.2
华丽	華麗	huálì	resplendent, splendid	5.5
滑铁卢	滑鐵盧	Huátiělú	Waterloo (a town in Belgium where Napoleon was defeated in 1815)	7.2
化		huà	to turn, transform	4.2
话音	話音	huàyīn	one's voice in speech	7.2
欢呼	歡呼	huānhū	to cheer, hail	4.2
环境	環境	huánjìng	environment, circumstances	5.1
荒郊		huāngjiāo	wilderness, wild countryside	5.1
皇冠		huángguān	royal crown	5.2
回音		huíyīn	reply, response	5.5
绘	繪	huì	to paint, describe	4.1
绘景	繪景	huìjǐng	scenery description	4.1
昏		hūn	dark, dim	5.1
浑厚	渾厚	húnhòu	(of voice) deep and resonant	6.2
活		huó	lively, vivid	3.1
活力		huólì	energy, vigor	7.2
火炉	火爐	huǒlú	(heating) stove, fireplace	6.4

J

击	擊	jī	to hit, beat	1.5
积	積	jī	to accumulate, store up	2.2
饥饿	饑餓	jī'è	hunger, starvation	6.4
基本		jīběn	basic, essential	1.5
基础	基礎	jīchǔ	base, basis	4.4
激动	激動	jīdòng	excited, enthusiastic	6.2
激发	激發	jīfā	to inspire, arouse, stimulate	7.1
基金		jījīn	fund	3.5
基金会	基金會	jījīnhuì	foundation	3.5
讥笑	譏笑	jīxiào	to ridicule	1.2
基于		jīyú	based on, on account of	7.2
即		jí	就是	7.1
即景生情		jíjǐng shēngqíng	the scene touches a chord in one's heart	5.3
吉祥		jíxiáng	lucky, auspicious	2.5
急需		jíxū	to be badly in need of	3.3

极致	極致	jízhì	perfection, highest attainments	5.3
急转直下	急轉直下	jízhuǎn zhíxià	a sudden turn for the worse	6.2
几时	幾時	jǐshí	when, what time	5.4
记录	記錄	jìlù	record, notes	6.5
纪念	紀念	jìniàn	to commemorate	2.5
纪念册	紀念冊	jìniàncè	commemorative album	2.5
技巧		jìqiǎo	technique, skill	6.1
记事	記事	jìshì	to remember things	3.2
记忆	記憶	jìyì	memorization	1.2
加		jiā	加拿大（简称）, abbreviation for Canada	4.2
加强	加強	jiāqiáng	to enhance, strengthen	7.4
加入		jiārù	to join, take part in	6.2
夹	夾	jiā	to mix, mingle, intersperse	7.5
夹叙夹议	夾敘夾議	jiāxù jiāyì	narration interspersed with comments	7.5
佳句		jiājù	beautiful line, well-formed sentence	5.4
驾照	駕照	jiàzhào	driver's license	3.2
坚持	堅持	jiānchí	to persist in, insist on	7.2
坚定	堅定	jiāndìng	firm, resolute	7.2
坚强	堅強	jiānqiáng	strong, firm	7.1
简洁	簡潔	jiǎnjié	terse, succinct	6.5
简历	簡歷	jiǎnlì	résumé	5.5
简明	簡明	jiǎnmíng	concise, simple, and clear	1.5
检验	檢驗	jiǎnyàn	to test, examine, inspect	7.2
简要	簡要	jiǎnyào	concise	6.5
键	鍵	jiàn	key (on a computer keyboard)	1.5
箭		jiàn	arrow	2.4
间接	間接	jiànjiē	indirect	1.1
建筑师	建築師	jiànzhùshī	architect	2.5
讲究	講究	jiǎngjiu	to be particular about, to stress	6.1
奖学金	獎學金	jiǎngxuéjīn	scholarship, fellowship	3.5
降		jiàng	to go down, fall; drop	4.2
降临	降臨	jiànglín	arrival (written language)	6.2
交代		jiāodài	to tell, account for	1.1
交流		jiāoliú	to exchange, interchange	6.2
交响乐	交響樂	jiāoxiǎngyuè	symphony	6.2
角度		jiǎodù	angle, point of view	4.2
皎洁	皎潔	jiǎojié	bright and clear	5.4
角落		jiǎoluò	corner	1.2
焦虑	焦慮	jiāolǜ	anxiety	6.4
脚印	腳印	jiǎoyìn	footprint	7.2
结	結	jié	to tie, knot	2.5
结构	結構	jiégòu	structure, composition	1.1
节目	節目	jiémù	program, item on a program	6.2
截然不同		jiérán bùtóng	entirely different	2.4
节奏	節奏	jiézòu	rhythm	5.3
解读	解讀	jiědú	interpretation, explanation	3.3
借用		jièyòng	to borrow, take	2.2
借助		jièzhù	to draw support from	6.1
金碧辉煌	金碧輝煌	jīnbì huīhuáng	(of a building, etc.) resplendent and magnificent	6.2
仅	僅	jǐn	只	7.2
紧凑	緊湊	jǐncòu	tight, well-knit, well-organized	1.3
尽可能	盡可能	jǐnkěnéng	as far as possible, to the best of one's ability	4.2
尽量	盡量	jǐnliàng	to the best of one's ability, as far as possible	6.5

紧密	緊密	jǐnmì	close together, inseparable	5.1
谨慎	謹慎	jǐnshèn	prudent, circumspect	7.2
进取心	進取心	jìnqǔxīn	enterprising spirit, desire to advance	7.1
经不住	經不住	jīngbùzhù	cannot withhold, must	1.2
经典	經典	jīngdiǎn	classics	2.2
经过	經過	jīngguò	process, course	1.1
惊叫	驚叫	jīngjiào	to scream, yell	4.2
经历	經歷	jīnglì	experience	1.2
精力		jīnglì	energy, vigor	5.2
精美		jīngměi	exquisite	4.5
精神抖擞	精神抖擻	jīngshén dǒusǒu	vigorous, energetic	1.2
精心		jīngxīn	painstakingly, elaborately	7.2
景观	景觀	jǐngguān	sights, landscape	4.1
景物		jǐngwù	scenery	4.1
景象		jǐngxiàng	scene, sight	4.2
境		jìng	border, boundary	4.2
境界		jìngjiè	realm, state	5.1
敬仰		jìngyǎng	to revere, venerate	6.2
九天		jiǔtiān	the Ninth Heaven, highest of heavens	4.2
菊花		júhuā	chrysanthemum	5.2
巨大		jùdà	huge, enormous	7.2
聚光灯	聚光燈	jùguāngdēng	spotlight	4.2
巨人		jùrén	giant	4.2
句式		jùshì	syntactical structure	7.4
具体	具體	jùtǐ	concrete, specific	2.1
具有		jùyǒu	to possess, have	1.4
绝对	絕對	juéduì	absolutely, definitely	7.2
军事	軍事	jūnshì	military affairs	7.2
骏马	駿馬	jùnmǎ	fine horse, steed	6.1

K

开掘	開掘	kāijué	to dig, (of literature) deeply explore and fully express	3.3
开门见山	開門見山	kāimén jiànshān	to be straight to the point, be upfront	5.5
开夜车	開夜車	kāiyèchē	to work late into the night	1.2
抗婚		kànghūn	to resist an arranged marriage	6.2
抗议	抗議	kàngyì	to protest	1.2
烤鹅	烤鵝	kǎo'é	roasted goose	6.4
考虑	考慮	kǎolǜ	to consider, deliberate	5.5
考验	考驗	kǎoyàn	test, trial	2.5
颗	顆	kē	*a measure word for grains and grain-like objects*	4.2
客观	客觀	kèguān	objective	5.1
刻画	刻畫	kèhuà	to depict, portray	2.1
肯定		kěndìng	certainly, surely	2.2
肯定		kěndìng	affirmation	7.2
坑		kēng	pit, hole	2.2
空缺		kōngquē	vacant position	5.5
口袋		kǒudài	pocket	1.2
扣		kòu	to button up, buckle, stick to	5.3
枯		kū	withered	5.1
枯燥		kūzào	dull and dry, uninteresting	2.1
苦寒		kǔhán	bitter cold	7.1
哭坟	哭墳	kūfén	to mourn (cry) at the tomb	6.3
夸张	誇張	kuāzhāng	exaggeration	4.2
快捷		kuàijié	quick, speedy	1.5
狂		kuáng	wild, violent	1.2

狂风大作	狂風大作	kuángfēng dàzuò	刮大风 the wind gusts	2.2
狂妄		kuángwàng	wildly arrogant, extremely conceited	7.2
狂笑		kuángxiào	to laugh wildly	1.2
魁		kuí	chief, head	7.2
困惑		kùnhuò	puzzled, confused	3.3
困难	困難	kùnnan	difficulty	7.1
扩张	擴張	kuòzhāng	to expand	7.2

L

垃圾		lājī	garbage, litter	1.2
喇叭		lǎba	trumpet, horn	2.2
狼狈	狼狽	lángbèi	in a difficult position; in a tight corner	2.3
琅琅上口		lángláng shàngkǒu	easy to read out	3.4
浪花		lànghuā	spray, spindrift	4.2
劳拉	勞拉	Láolā	Laura	1.2
老子		Lǎozǐ	Laozi, founder of Daoism	2.1
雷		léi	thunder	2.2
类	類	lèi	kind, type	7.4
类似	類似	lèisì	similar	1.3
梨		lí	pear	3.4
李白		lǐbái	poet (701–762)	4.2
立即		lìjí	immediately	2.2
例如		lìrú	for example	7.4
丽莎	麗莎	Lìshā	Lisa	1.2
连忙	連忙	liánmáng	hastily, promptly	1.2
联系	聯繫	liánxì	to contact, connect	5.5
联想	聯想	liánxiǎng	association, connection of ideas, feelings, etc.	5.3
练	練	liàn	white silk	4.2
梁		liáng	beam	1.2
梁山伯		Liáng Shānbó	personal name	6.2
梁祝		Liángzhù	Butterfly Lovers (title of a violin concerto)	6.2
量体温	量體溫	liángtǐwēn	to take one's temperature	3.2
两者	兩者	liǎngzhě	the two sides	7.2
了结	了結	liǎojié	to finish, settle up	3.5
料		liào	to expect, anticipate	2.2
列		liè	to list	6.5
琳达	琳達	Líndá	Linda	1.2
灵活	靈活	línghuó	nimble, flexible	6.1
令人		lìngrén	使人 render, make someone	7.3
令人神往		lìngrén shénwǎng	to cause a craving for, have a strong appeal	5.2
令人信服		lìngrén xìnfú	convincing	7.3
另一番		lìngyīfān	different, another kind of	4.2
流放		liúfàng	to exile, banish	7.2
留恋	留戀	liúliàn	(of feeling) lingering, attached	6.2
流露		liúlù	to reveal, to show unintentionally	6.1
柳树	柳樹	liǔshù	willow	6.2
露		lù	to reveal, show	3.2
路况	路況	lùkuàng	road condition	2.3
旅途		lǚtú	journey, trip	2.5
轮	輪	lún	wheel, *measure word for the full moon and the sun*	5.4
论点	論點	lùndiǎn	argument, thesis, point of view	7.1
论据	論據	lùnjù	grounds of argument, supporting material	7.1

批驳	批駁	pībó	to criticize, refute	7.3
劈头盖脸	劈頭蓋臉	pītóu gàiliǎn	right in the face	4.2
篇幅		piānfu	length of an article	3.5
飘	飄	piāo	to flutter, float	5.2
瓢		piáo	gourd ladle	4.2
瓢泼大雨	瓢潑大雨	piáopō dàyǔ	pouring rain	4.2
品格		pǐngé	character, personality	2.3
平淡		píngdàn	dull, uninteresting	2.1
评估	評估	pínggū	evaluation, estimate	7.2
评论	評論	pínglùn	commentary, review, critique	7.5
屏幕		píngmù	screen	1.5
平台		píngtái	terrace, platform	4.2
评委	評委	píngwěi	judge, member of a panel of judges	7.2
评委会	評委會	píngwěihuì	panel of judges	7.2
平行		píngxíng	parallel	7.1
泼	潑	pō	to splash, spill	4.2
破产	破產	pòchǎn	bankruptcy	1.2
剖析		pōuxī	to analyze, dissect	7.1
铺	鋪	pū	to spread, lay, pave	5.2
朴素	樸素	pǔsù	simple, plain	6.5
普通		pǔtōng	common, ordinary	3.1
瀑		pù	waterfall	4.2
瀑布		pùbù	waterfall	4.2
瀑布后之旅	瀑布後之旅	pùbùhòuzhīlǚ	"Journey behind the Falls"	4.2

Q

凄凉	淒涼	qīliáng	bleak, desolate; miserable	5.1
期终	期終	qīzhōng	end of the semester	1.2
其		qí	his, her, its, their	7.5
其次		qícì	next, secondly	7.5
其中		qízhōng	among (which, them, etc.)	4.2
起		qǐ	to start, begin, initiate	7.3
启发	啓發	qǐfā	to inspire, arouse	5.4
起伏		qǐfú	rise and fall	6.3
启示	啓示	qǐshì	enlightenment, inspiration	7.5
企业	企業	qǐyè	enterprise, business	6.5
起因		qǐyīn	cause, reason	1.1
起作用		qǐ zuòyòng	to play a part	1.3
砌		qì	to lay bricks or stones	5.2
泣		qì	to weep, sob	6.2
气氛	氣氛	qìfēn	atmosphere	6.2
气势	氣勢	qìshì	momentum, impetus	3.4
气味	氣味	qìwèi	smell, scent	4.1
气息	氣息	qìxī	tinge, atmosphere	1.3
牵	牽	qiān	to pull, draw	5.1
千变万化	千變萬化	qiānbiàn wànhuà	ever-changing	4.2
千古		qiāngǔ	through the ages	5.4
谦虚	謙虛	qiānxū	modest, humble	7.2
强烈	強烈	qiángliè	strong, powerful, intense	3.4
乔迁	喬遷	qiáoqiān	to move to a better place	2.5
巧妙		qiǎomiào	ingenious, smart, clever	4.4
翘	翹	qiào	to curl up, stick up	3.2
亲切	親切	qīnqiè	warm, close, affectionate	5.5
琴		qín	general name for certain musical instruments	6.2
倾	傾	qīng	to overturn and pour out	2.2
倾盆大雨	傾盆大雨	qīngpéndàyǔ	heavy downpour, torrential rain	2.2

轻飘	輕飄	qīngpiāo	light, fluffy	4.2
轻视	輕視	qīngshì	to despise, look down	7.2
倾听	傾聽	qīngtīng	to listen attentively to	3.3
倾泻	傾瀉	qīngxiè	to rush down in torrent, pour down	4.2
清醒		qīngxǐng	sober, clear-headed	1.2
轻盈	輕盈	qīngyíng	lighthearted and melodious	6.2
情节	情節	qíngjié	plot, details of a story	2.1
情景交融		qíngjǐng jiāoróng	(of literary work) fusion of the feelings with the natural settings	5.1
秋菊傲霜		qiūjú àoshuāng	the autumn chrysanthemum braves the frost	5.2
求职	求職	qiúzhí	to seek a position, apply for a job	5.5
区别	區別	qūbié	difference	7.2
区分	區分	qūfēn	to differentiate, distinguish	7.2
曲折		qūzhé	complication, intricacy	6.2
曲		qǔ	song, tune, melody	2.2
圈		quān	circle, ring	5.2
圈套		quāntào	trap, snare	7.2
泉		quán	spring, fountain	3.2
全景		quánjǐng	panorama	5.3
权威人士	權威人士	quánwēi rénshì	authoritative people	7.2
缺乏		quēfá	to be short of, lack	7.2
缺课	缺課	quēkè	to be absent from class	3.3
群		qún	swarm, group	5.2
群众	群衆	qúnzhòng	mass, common people, general public	4.5

R

染		rǎn	to dye, tint	5.2
热烈	熱烈	rèliè	enthusiastic, ardent	6.1
人格		réngé	personality, character	5.4
柔和		róuhé	soft, gentle	5.2
如泣如诉	如泣如訴	rúqì rúsù	(of music) very pathetic and touching	6.2

S

塞		sāi	to stuff, squeeze in	1.2
嗓子		sǎngzi	throat, voice	4.4
色泽	色澤	sèzé	color and luster	2.5
闪电	閃電	shǎndiàn	lightning	2.2
善于		shànyú	to be good at	4.1
少年		shàonián	early youth	1.1
舍		shě	to give up, abandon	6.2
设计	設計	shèjì	design	4.5
社团	社團	shètuán	mass organizations, association	4.5
深沉	深沈	shēnchén	(of feeling) deep	6.2
深化		shēnhuà	to deepen, reinforce	2.1
身经百战	身經百戰	shēnjīng bǎizhàn	to be a veteran in battle, be battle-seasoned	1.2
深刻		shēnkè	deep, profound	2.3
申请	申請	shēnqǐng	application	5.5
神奇		shénqí	magical, wonderful	4.2
神态	神態	shéntài	expression, manner, bearing	1.4
渗透	滲透	shèntòu	to permeate	5.1
升华	升華	shēnghuá	sublimation	6.2
生机	生機	shēngjī	life, vigor, vitality	5.2
声响	聲響	shēngxiǎng	sound	4.1
省略		shěnglüè	to omit, skip	1.5
盛		shèng	vigorous, energetic	3.4

T

台侧	台側	táicè	side stage	3.2
滩	灘	tān	a puddle of, a pool of	2.2
掏		tāo	to take out, draw out	1.2
桃		táo	peach	3.4
特征		tèzhēng	feature, trait	3.1
藤		téng	vine	5.1
提出		tíchū	to put forward, set forth, propose	6.4
提供		tígòng	to provide, supply	3.3
提示		tíshì	guide, cue	1.2
题写	題寫	tíxiě	to write, inscribe	2.5
体温表	體溫表	tǐwēnbiǎo	clinical thermometer	3.2
天才		tiāncái	genius, talent	7.2
天蓝	天藍	tiānlán	sky-blue, azure	4.2
天下		tiānxià	land under heaven, world	2.1
天涯		tiānyá	end of the world; remotest place on earth	5.1
田野		tiányě	field	5.2
调节	調節	tiáojié	adjustment	5.2
条文	條文	tiáowén	article, clause	1.2
贴切	貼切	tiēqiè	(of words) appropriate, proper	3.3
通常		tōngcháng	generally, commonly, usually	4.5
通篇		tōngpiān	throughout the essay	5.3
通俗		tōngsú	popular, common, simple	2.4
通宵		tōngxiāo	all night, throughout the night	1.2
铜	銅	tóng	copper, bronze	4.4
童话	童話	tónghuà	children's story, fairy tale	6.4
同情		tóngqíng	to sympathize	6.4
痛快		tòngkuài	very joyful, to one's great satisfaction	1.2
头脑	頭腦	tóunǎo	brain; mind	1.2
透彻	透徹	tòuchè	penetrating, thorough	3.4
透出		tòuchū	to reveal, show	3.3
突出		tūchū	protruding, projecting	4.2
图	圖	tú	to pursue, seek	1.5
涂	塗	tú	to apply, smear	4.1
推荐	推薦	tuījiàn	to recommend, nominate	3.5

W

外貌		wàimào	appearance, looks	3.1
晚霞		wǎnxiá	sunset glow, sunset clouds	6.2
婉转	婉轉	wǎnzhuǎn	mild and indirect	6.2
万事如意	萬事如意	wànshìrúyì	everything goes as one wishes, "May all go well with you!"	2.5
网络	網絡	wǎngluò	network	4.5
威	威	wēi	power, strength	2.3
微微		wēiwēi	slight, faint	3.2
微笑		wēixiào	smile	3.2
围	圍	wéi	to enclose, surround	5.2
为	爲	wéi	成	7.1
畏		wèi	to fear	5.2
文笔	文筆	wénbǐ	style of writing	1.1
文雅		wényǎ	elegant, refined	4.3
文艺	文藝	wényì	literature and art	4.5
稳	穩	wěn	steady, stable	2.2
乌云	烏雲	wūyún	dark clouds	2.2
无数	無數	wúshù	innumerable, countless	1.2
无知	無知	wúzhī	ignorance	7.2

五彩缤纷	五彩繽紛	wǔcǎi bīnfēn	colorful	4.2
五大湖		wǔdàhú	the Great Lakes	4.2
五颜六色	五顏六色	wǔyánliùsè	colorful	4.2
午夜		wǔyè	midnight	1.2
物		wù	thing, object	1.4
雾	霧	wù	fog	4.1
物品		wùpǐn	goods	3.3

X

溪		xī	stream, brook	2.2
夕		xī	sunset	5.1
夕阳	夕陽	xīyáng	the setting sun	5.1
吸引		xīyǐn	to attract	4.5
西游记	西遊記	xīyóujì	*Journey to the West*	4.2
席		xí	seat	3.2
席地而坐		xídì érzuò	to sit on the ground or floor	5.2
喜悦	喜悅	xǐyuè	happy, joyous	6.1
细	細	xì	小 tiny, trivial	2.1
细节	細節	xìjié	detail	2.1
细腻	細膩	xìnì	delicate, exquisite	2.1
细微	細微	xìwēi	subtle, slight	2.1
细致	細致	xìzhì	careful, exquisite	3.4
霞		xiá	rosy clouds, morning or evening glow	3.4
吓	嚇	xià	to scare, frighten	1.2
下列		xiàliè	listed or mentioned below, following	7.1
下马威	下馬威	xiàmǎwēi	show of strength at first contact	2.3
仙		xiān	immortal, fairy	4.2
仙境		xiānjìng	fairyland, wonderland	4.2
鲜明	鮮明	xiānmíng	distinct, striking	2.4
弦		xián	bowstring, string	2.4
显得	顯得	xiǎnde	to seem, look, appear	2.1
显示	顯示	xiǎnshì	to show, demonstrate	7.1
线	線	xiàn	thread, string	2.4
现实	現實	xiànshí	reality	4.4
线索	線索	xiànsuǒ	clue, thread	1.3
限制		xiànzhì	restriction, limit	7.2
相关	相關	xiāngguān	related, interrelated	3.4
相通		xiāngtōng	interlinked	2.4
像......般		xiàng ... bān	same as, just like	2.2
潇洒	瀟灑	xiāosǎ	natural and elegant	6.2
消失		xiāoshī	to disappear, vanish	3.2
消息		xiāoxi	news, message	4.5
小品		xiǎopǐn	skit	2.2
小提琴		xiǎotíqín	violin	6.2
小泽征尔	小澤征爾	xiǎozé zhēng'ěr	Seiji Ozawa (b. 1935), a Japanese-American conductor	7.2
效果		xiàoguǒ	effect, result	3.4
笑容		xiàoróng	smiling expression, smile	3.2
笑意		xiàoyì	faint smile	3.2
协奏曲	協奏曲	xiézòuqǔ	concerto	6.2
心理		xīnlǐ	psychology, mind	5.4
新娘面纱	新娘面紗	xīnniáng miànshā	"Bridal Veil Falls"	4.2
欣赏	欣賞	xīnshǎng	to enjoy, appreciate	6.2
心弦		xīnxián	heartstrings	6.2
心心相印		xīnxīn xiāngyìn	to have mutual love and affinity	6.2
新颖	新穎	xīnyǐng	new, novel	4.5
信服		xìnfú	to be convinced	7.3

信号	信號	xìnhào	signal	2.2
信心		xìnxīn	confidence	7.2
行道树	行道樹	xíngdào shù	roadside or sidewalk trees	1.4
形容词	形容詞	xíngróngcí	adjective	4.2
形态	形態	xíngtài	shape, form	4.1
形象		xíngxiàng	image, figure	1.4
杏		xìng	apricot	3.4
雄伟	雄偉	xióngwéi	majestic	4.2
修辞	修辭	xiūcí	rhetoric	1.4
休整		xiūzhěng	rest and reorganization	5.2
悬	懸	xuán	挂, to hang	1.2
悬梁刺股	懸梁刺股	xuánliáng cìgǔ	to tie one's hair on the house beam and jab one's thigh with an awl to keep oneself awake – painstaking in one's study	1.2
悬念	懸念	xuánniàn	suspense	1.1
选择	選擇	xuǎnzé	to choose, select	5.1
绚丽	絢麗	xuànlì	bright and colorful, gorgeous	5.2
学术	學術	xuéshù	learning, academics	4.5
学子	學子	xuézǐ	学生 student	1.2
迅速		xùnsù	quick, rapid, swift	5.5

Y

鸦	鴉	yā	crow	5.1
压台	壓台	yātái	grand finale of a theatrical performance, last and the most important item	6.2
研究院		yánjiūyuàn	research institute, graduate school	6.5
严密	嚴密	yánmì	accurate, tight, well-knit	7.1
言行		yánxíng	words and deeds, speech, and action	1.4
演出		yǎnchū	show, performance	4.5
眼角		yǎnjiǎo	corner of the eye	3.2
眼看		yǎnkàn	soon, shortly	2.2
眼皮		yǎnpí	eyelids	1.2
眼球		yǎnqiú	eyeball	4.5
演绎	演繹	yǎnyì	deduction, inference	7.1
演奏		yǎnzòu	to play a musical instrument	7.2
扬琴	揚琴	yángqín	dulcimer	6.2
要点	要點	yàodiǎn	key point, essentials	1.5
要素		yàosù	key element	1.1
夜宵		yèxiāo	midnight snack	1.2
一般		yībān	一样 same	1.2
一不小心		yībù xiǎoxīn	with a reckless negligence	1.2
一度		yīdù	once, at one time	7.2
一目了然		yīmù liǎorán	to see clearly at a glance	6.5
一切		yīqiè	all, every	7.2
疑		yí	to suspect	4.2
疑惑		yíhuò	doubt	2.2
宜人		yírén	pleasant, delightful	5.2
以及		yǐjí	along with, as well as	4.5
以...为序	以...爲序	yǐ...wéixù	in order of	1.1
以下		yǐxià	below, the following	5.5
异	異	yì	different	5.1
议论	議論	yìlùn	comment, discussion	6.1
议论文	議論文	yìlùnwén	persuasive writing	7.1
译名	譯名	yìmíng	translated name or term	2.2
意志		yìzhì	will	7.1

音调	音調	yīndiào	tone	6.2
因人而异	因人而異	yīnrén éryì	differ from person to person	5.1
音乐剧	音樂劇	yīnyuèjù	musical	2.2
音乐厅	音樂廳	yīnyuètīng	concert hall	6.2
银	銀	yín	silver	2.5
银河	銀河	yínhé	the Milky Way	4.2
引		yǐn	to cause, arouse, trigger	5.2
引起		yǐnqǐ	to cause, arouse, generate	7.4
引人入胜	引人入勝	yǐnrénrùshèng	to lead one into the interesting part of something, alluring, fascinating	1.1
引用		yǐnyòng	to cite, quote	4.4
应	應	yīng	应该 should	6.5
迎接		yíngjiē	to greet, welcome	3.2
映衬	映襯	yìngchèn	to set off, relieve against	5.2
映射		yìngshè	to shine upon	6.2
应用	應用	yìngyòng	to use, apply	1.5
应用文	應用文	yìngyòngwén	practical writing	1.5
永恒		yǒnghéng	eternity	5.4
忧伤	憂傷	yōushāng	distressed	6.2
优势	優勢	yōushì	advantage, strength, superiority	6.5
优雅	優雅	yōuyǎ	elegant, graceful	6.2
游记	遊記	yóujì	travel notes, travel journal	4.2
有理		yǒulǐ	reasonable, justified	1.2
有力		yǒulì	strong, powerful	7.3
有所不同		yǒusuǒ bùtóng	有点不一样 slightly different	6.5
有效		yǒuxiào	effective, valid	3.1
余波		yúbō	repercussions, aftermath	2.3
雨点	雨點	yǔdiǎn	raindrop	2.2
宇宙		yǔzhòu	universe, cosmos	5.4
寓		yù	to imply, contain	5.1
愈加		yùjiā	increasingly, even more	2.5
寓情于景		yùqíng yújǐng	to imply feelings in a scene	5.1
预示	預示	yùshì	to foreshow, betoken, indicate	6.2
元代		Yuándài	Yuan Dynasty (1271–1368)	5.1
原来	原來	yuánlái	as it turns out	7.2
圆满	圓滿	yuánmǎn	satisfactory, perfect	5.4
原由		yuányóu	cause, reason	3.5
原作		yuánzuò	original work	7.5
乐谱	樂譜	yuèpǔ	music score, sheet music, music	7.2
乐器	樂器	yuèqì	musical instrument	6.2
乐曲	樂曲	yuèqǔ	musical composition	2.2
韵	韻	yùn	beautiful or sweet sound, appeal, charm	6.2
蕴含	蘊含	yùnhán	to contain, imply	6.2
运用	運用	yùnyòng	to utilize, apply	4.4

Z

赞美	贊美	zànměi	to admire, praise	5.2
赞叹	贊歎	zàntàn	to gasp in admiration, praise highly	5.2
则	則	zé	yet, though	4.2
增强	增強	zēngqiáng	to strengthen, enhance	3.4
增添		zēngtiān	to add, increase	5.2
眨		zhǎ	to blink, wink	1.4
摘取		zhāiqǔ	to pick, pluck	7.2
沾		zhān	to be stained with	2.2
展		zhǎn	to put to good use, give free play to	2.5
绽放	綻放	zhànfàng	to blossom	5.2